Chapter 1 — Basic number

1 Find the row and column sums of each of these grids.

a

2	5	1	☐
8	3	4	☐
9	7	6	☐
☐	☐	☐	☐

b

3	0	1	☐
7	5	6	☐
8	4	2	☐
☐	☐	☐	☐

c

0	3	5	☐
9	6	8	☐
2	7	1	☐
☐	☐	☐	☐

d

3	1	8	☐
6	2	0	☐
7	9	4	☐
☐	☐	☐	☐

e

8	1	3	☐
6	4	5	☐
2	7	0	☐
☐	☐	☐	☐

2 Find the numbers missing from each of these grids. Remember: the numbers missing from each grid must be chosen from 0 to 9 without any repeats.

a

1	5	☐	10
8	☐	7	17
☐	9	6	18
12	16	17	45

b

4	☐	5	10
☐	6	☐	8
7	8	☐	18
13	15	8	36

c

☐	☐	☐	14
0	9	8	17
2	☐	5	10
9	18	14	☐

d

4	☐	☐	12
☐	0	5	12
☐	8	3	☐
12	☐	10	36

e

☐	☐	3	10
☐	0	☐	☐
8	2	☐	15
16	☐	12	☐

1 Write down the answer to each of the following without looking at a multiplication square.

a 4×3 **b** 7×4 **c** 6×5 **d** 3×8 **e** 8×6
f 9×4 **g** 5×9 **h** 9×7 **i** 8×8 **j** 9×8
k 7×6 **l** 7×7 **m** 4×6 **n** 8×7 **o** 5×5

2 Write down the answer to each of the following without looking at a multiplication square.

a $14 \div 2$ **b** $28 \div 4$ **c** $24 \div 6$ **d** $20 \div 5$ **e** $18 \div 3$
f $35 \div 5$ **g** $27 \div 3$ **h** $32 \div 4$ **i** $24 \div 8$ **j** $21 \div 7$
k $42 \div 6$ **l** $40 \div 8$ **m** $18 \div 9$ **n** $49 \div 7$ **o** $48 \div 6$

3 Write down the answer to each of the following. Look carefully at the signs, because they are a mixture of +, −, × and ÷.

a $8 + 5$ **b** $20 - 6$ **c** 4×5 **d** $16 \div 4$ **e** $14 - 8$
f $15 \div 3$ **g** $16 + 8$ **h** 5×7 **i** $16 + 5$ **j** $36 \div 6$
k $17 - 8$ **l** 9×3 **m** $42 \div 7$ **n** 6×9 **o** $21 - 6$

4 Write down the answer to each of the following.

a 4×10 **b** 7×10 **c** 9×10 **d** 11×10 **e** 3×100
f 5×100 **g** 24×100 **h** 45×100 **i** $80 \div 10$ **j** $130 \div 10$
k $510 \div 10$ **l** $1000 \div 10$ **m** $700 \div 100$ **n** $900 \div 100$ **o** $1200 \div 100$

CW00349348

1 Work out each of these.

a $3 \times 4 + 7 =$ b $8 + 2 \times 4 =$ c $12 \div 3 + 4 =$ d $10 - 8 \div 2 =$

e $7 + 2 - 3 =$ f $5 \times 4 - 8 =$ g $9 + 10 \div 5 =$ h $11 - 9 \div 1 =$

i $12 \div 1 - 6 =$ j $4 + 4 \times 4 =$

2 Work out each of these. Remember: first work out the bracket.

a $3 \times (2 + 4) =$ b $12 \div (4 + 2) =$ c $(4 + 6) \div 5 =$

d $(10 - 6) + 5 =$ e $3 \times (9 \div 3) =$ f $5 + (4 \times 2) =$

g $(5 + 3) \div 2 =$ h $(5 \div 1) \times 4 =$ i $(7 - 4) \times (1 + 4) =$

j $(7 + 5) \div (6 - 3) =$

3 Copy each of these and then put in brackets to make each sum true.

a $4 \times 5 - 1 = 16$ b $8 \div 2 + 4 = 8$ c $8 - 3 \times 4 = 20$ d $12 - 5 \times 2 = 2$

e $3 \times 3 + 2 = 15$ f $12 \div 2 + 1 = 4$ g $9 \times 6 \div 3 = 18$ h $20 - 8 + 5 = 7$

i $6 + 4 \div 2 = 5$ j $16 \div 4 \div 2 = 8$

4 Put any of $+, -, \times, \div$ or ( ) in each sum to make it true.

a $2 \quad 5 \quad 10 = 0$ b $10 \quad 2 \quad 5 = 1$ c $10 \quad 5 \quad 2 = 3$ d $10 \quad 2 \quad 5 = 4$

e $10 \quad 5 \quad 2 = 7$ f $5 \quad 10 \quad 2 = 10$ g $10 \quad 5 \quad 2 = 13$ h $5 \quad 10 \quad 2 = 17$

i $10 \quad 2 \quad 5 = 20$ j $5 \quad 10 \quad 2 = 25$

5 Amanda worked out $3 + 4 \times 5$ and got the answer 35. Andrew worked out $3 + 4 \times 5$ and got the answer 23. Explain why they got different answers.

1 Write the value of each underlined digit.

a   5<u>7</u>6   b   37<u>4</u>   c   <u>6</u>89   d   <u>4</u>785   e   300<u>7</u>

f   7<u>6</u>08   g   354<u>2</u>   h   1<u>2</u>745   i   <u>8</u>7 409   j   <u>7</u> 777 777

2 Write each of the following using just words.

a   7245   b   9072   c   29 450   d   2 760 000

3 Write each of the following using digits only.

a   Eight thousand and five hundred   b   Forty two thousand and forty two

c   Six million   d   Five million and five.

4 Write these numbers in order, putting the **smallest** first.

a   31, 20, 14, 22, 8, 25, 30, 12

b   159, 155, 176, 167, 170, 168, 151, 172

c   2100, 2070, 2002, 1990, 2010, 1998, 2000, 2092

5 Write these numbers in order, putting the **largest** first.

a   49, 62, 75, 57, 50, 72

b   988, 1052, 999, 1010, 980, 1007

c   4567, 4765, 4675, 4576, 4657, 4756

6 Using each of the digits 7, 8 and 9 only once in each number:

a   Write as many three-digit numbers as you can.

b   Which of your numbers is the smallest?

c   Which of your numbers is the largest?

7 Write down in order of size, largest first, all the two-digit numbers that can be made using 2, 4 and 6. (Each digit can be repeated.)

8 Copy each of these sentences, writing the numbers in words.
    a The diameter of the Earth at the equator is 12 756 kilometres.
    b The Moon is approximately 238 000 miles from the Earth.
    c The greatest distance of the Earth from the Sun is 94 600 000 miles.

HOMEWORK 1E

1 Round off each of these numbers to the nearest 10.
    a 34   **b** 67   **c** 23   **d** 49   **e** 55
    f 11   **g** 95   **h** 123   **i** 109   **j** 125

2 Round off each of these numbers to the nearest 100.
    a 231   **b** 389   **c** 410   **d** 777   **e** 850
    f 117   **g** 585   **h** 250   **i** 975   **j** 1245

3 Round off each of these numbers to the nearest 1000.
    a 2176   **b** 3800   **c** 6760   **d** 4455   **e** 1204
    f 6782   **g** 5500   **h** 8808   **i** 1500   **j** 9999

4 Give these bus journey times to the nearest 5 minutes.
    a 16 minutes   **b** 28 minutes   **c** 34 minutes   **d** 42 minutes
    e $23\frac{1}{2}$ minutes   **f** $17\frac{1}{2}$ minutes

5 The selling prices of five houses in a village is as follows:

FOR SALE £8400	FOR SALE £12 900	FOR SALE £45 300	FOR SALE £75 550	FOR SALE £99 500

Give the prices to the nearest thousand pounds.

6 Mark knows that he has £240 in his savings account to the nearest ten pounds.
    a What is the smallest amount that he could have?
    b What is the greatest amount that he could have?

7 The size of a crowd at an open air pop festival was reported to be 8000 to the nearest thousand.
    a What is the lowest number that the crowd could be?
    b What is the largest number that the crowd could be?

HOMEWORK 1F

1 Copy and work out each of these additions.
    a 75 + 23   **b** 245 + 156   **c** 307 + 293   **d** 4158 + 3951   **e** 4289 532 + 96

2 Complete each of these additions.
    a 25 + 89 + 12   **b** 211 + 385 + 46   **c** 125 + 88 + 720
    d 478 + 207 + 300   **e** 1275 + 3245 + 524

3 Copy and complete each of these subtractions.

a	354	**b**	651	**c**	785	**d**	450	**e**	5421
	−120		−128		−207		−178		−2568

4 Complete each of these subtractions.

a 386 − 296   **b** 709 − 518   **c** 452 − 386

d 800 − 258   **e** 7208 − 1564

5 Copy each of these and fill in the missing digits.

a	4 5	**b**	□7	**c**	3 □ 4	**d**	□ □ □
	+3 □		+4 □		+2 8 6		+ 2 8 7
	□7		9 2		□ 4 □		5 5 5

6 Copy each of these and fill in the missing digits.

a	7 5	**b**	3 2 □	**c**	5 8 3	**d**	□ □ □
	− 1 □		−1 □ 4		−□ □ □		− 2 4 8
	□3		1 8 2		1 3 5		3 7 4

 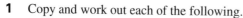

HOMEWORK 1G

1 Copy and work out each of the following.

a	24	**b**	38	**c**	124	**d**	408	**e**	359
	× 3		× 4		× 5		× 6		× 8

2 Calculate each of these multiplications.

a 21×5 **b** 37×7 **c** 203×9 **d** 4×876 **e** 6×3214

3 By doing a suitable multiplication, answer each of these questions.
    a How many people could seven 55-seater coaches hold?
    b Adam buys seven postcards at 23p each. How much does he spend?
    c Nails are packed in boxes of 144. How many nails are there in five boxes?
    d Eight people book a holiday, costing £284 each. What is the total cost?
    e How many yards are there in six miles if there are 1760 yards in a mile?

4 Calculate each of these divisions.

a $684 \div 2$ **b** $525 \div 3$ **c** $804 \div 4$ **d** $7260 \div 5$ **e** $2560 \div 8$

5 By doing a suitable division, answer each of these questions.
    a In a school there are 288 students in 8 forms in Year 10. If there are the same number of students in each form, how many students are there in each one?
    b Phil jogs seven miles every morning. How many days will it take him to cover a total distance of 441 miles?
    c In a supermarket cans of cola are sold in packs of six. If there are 750 cans on the shelf, how many packs are there?
    d Sandra's wages for a month were £2060. How much does she earn in a week?
    e Tickets for a charity disco were sold at £5 each? How many people bought tickets if the total sales were £1710?

Chapter 2 — Fractions

  HOMEWORK 2A

1 What fraction is shaded in each of these diagrams?

a   **b**   **c**

d    **e**   **f**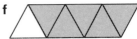

g   **h**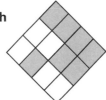

2 Draw diagrams as in Question **1** to show these fractions.

   a $\frac{1}{3}$ **b** $\frac{3}{5}$ **c** $\frac{7}{10}$ **d** $\frac{5}{8}$ **e** $\frac{7}{9}$

   f $\frac{3}{7}$ **g** $\frac{5}{12}$ **h** $\frac{7}{15}$

 HOMEWORK 2B

Example   **a** $\frac{5}{12} + \frac{4}{12} = \frac{9}{12}$

              b $\frac{7}{10} - \frac{3}{10} = \frac{4}{10}$

1 Calculate each of the following.

   a $\frac{1}{4} + \frac{1}{4}$ **b** $\frac{2}{5} + \frac{1}{5}$ **c** $\frac{3}{7} + \frac{2}{7}$ **d** $\frac{5}{8} + \frac{1}{8}$ **e** $\frac{3}{6} + \frac{2}{6}$

   f $\frac{4}{9} + \frac{4}{9}$ **g** $\frac{3}{10} + \frac{4}{10}$ **h** $\frac{2}{5} + \frac{2}{5}$ **i** $\frac{4}{12} + \frac{1}{12}$ **j** $\frac{5}{20} + \frac{7}{20}$

2 Calculate each of the following.

   a $\frac{4}{5} - \frac{2}{5}$ **b** $\frac{5}{8} - \frac{1}{8}$ **c** $\frac{6}{7} - \frac{2}{7}$ **d** $\frac{8}{10} - \frac{3}{10}$ **e** $\frac{5}{6} - \frac{3}{6}$

   f $\frac{7}{9} - \frac{3}{9}$ **g** $\frac{7}{8} - \frac{1}{8}$ **h** $\frac{4}{9} - \frac{2}{9}$ **i** $\frac{7}{12} - \frac{5}{12}$ **j** $\frac{11}{20} - \frac{3}{20}$

3 **a** Draw two diagrams to show $\frac{4}{8}$ and $\frac{2}{8}$.

    b Show on your diagrams that $\frac{4}{8} = \frac{1}{2}$ and $\frac{2}{8} = \frac{1}{4}$.

    c Use the above information to write down the answers to

       i $\frac{1}{2} + \frac{1}{8}$ **ii** $\frac{1}{2} + \frac{3}{8}$ **iii** $\frac{1}{4} + \frac{1}{8}$ **iv** $\frac{3}{4} + \frac{1}{8}$ **v** $\frac{1}{2} - \frac{1}{8}$ **vi** $\frac{1}{2} - \frac{3}{8}$ **vii** $\frac{1}{4} - \frac{1}{8}$ **viii** $\frac{3}{4} - \frac{1}{8}$

1 Copy the diagram and use it to write down each of these fractions as tenths.

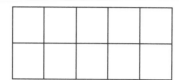

a $\frac{1}{2}$ b $\frac{1}{5}$ c $\frac{2}{5}$ d $\frac{3}{5}$ e $\frac{4}{5}$

2 Use your answers to Question **1** to write down the answer to each of the following. Each answer will be so many tenths.

a $\frac{1}{2}+\frac{1}{5}$ b $\frac{1}{2}+\frac{3}{10}$ c $\frac{2}{5}+\frac{1}{10}$ d $\frac{1}{5}+\frac{7}{10}$ e $\frac{1}{2}-\frac{2}{5}$ f $\frac{9}{10}-\frac{3}{5}$

3 Copy the diagram and use it to write down each of these fractions as twelfths.

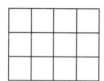

a $\frac{1}{2}$ b $\frac{1}{4}$ c $\frac{1}{3}$ d $\frac{3}{4}$ e $\frac{2}{3}$

4 Use your answers to Question **3** to write down the answer to each of the following. Each answer will be so many twelfths.

a $\frac{1}{2}+\frac{1}{3}$ b $\frac{1}{4}+\frac{1}{3}$ c $\frac{2}{3}+\frac{1}{4}$ d $\frac{1}{4}+\frac{7}{12}$ e $\frac{5}{12}+\frac{1}{2}$

f $\frac{2}{3}-\frac{1}{2}$ g $\frac{3}{4}-\frac{1}{3}$ h $\frac{1}{2}-\frac{1}{12}$ i $\frac{3}{4}-\frac{5}{12}$ j $\frac{2}{3}-\frac{7}{12}$

Example 1   Show $\frac{2}{3}$ is equivalent to $\frac{8}{12}$.

$$\frac{2}{3} \ \blacktriangleright \ \frac{\times 4}{\times 4} = \frac{8}{12}$$

Example 2   Cancel down $\frac{15}{20}$ to its simplest form.

$$\frac{15}{20} \ \blacktriangleright \ \frac{\div 5}{\div 5} = \frac{3}{4}$$

Example 3   Put these fractions in order with the smallest first: $\frac{5}{6}$ $\frac{2}{3}$ $\frac{3}{4}$.

By equivalent fractions $\frac{5}{6}=\frac{10}{12}$ $\frac{2}{3}=\frac{8}{12}$ $\frac{3}{4}=\frac{9}{12}$

Putting in order: $\frac{2}{3}$ $\frac{3}{4}$ $\frac{5}{6}$

1 Copy and complete each of these statements.

a $\frac{1}{4} \ \blacktriangleright \ \frac{\times 3}{\times 3} = \frac{}{12}$ b $\frac{3}{5} \ \blacktriangleright \ \frac{\times 4}{\times 4} = \frac{}{20}$ c $\frac{5}{8} \ \blacktriangleright \ \frac{\times 2}{\times 2} = \frac{}{16}$ d $\frac{4}{7} \ \blacktriangleright \ \frac{\times 3}{\times 3} = \frac{12}{}$

e $\frac{2}{3} \ \blacktriangleright \ \frac{\times}{\times 5} = \frac{}{15}$ f $\frac{5}{9} \ \blacktriangleright \ \frac{\times}{\times 2} = \frac{}{18}$ g $\frac{6}{7} \ \blacktriangleright \ \frac{\times}{\times} = \frac{}{35}$ h $\frac{1}{10} \ \blacktriangleright \ \frac{\times}{\times} = \frac{}{40}$

2 Copy and complete each of these statements.

a $\quad\dfrac{1}{4} = \dfrac{2}{8} = \dfrac{}{12} = \dfrac{4}{} = \dfrac{}{20} = \dfrac{6}{24}$

b $\quad\dfrac{2}{3} = \dfrac{4}{6} = \dfrac{}{} = \dfrac{}{12} = \dfrac{10}{} = \dfrac{12}{18}$

c $\quad\dfrac{4}{5} = \dfrac{}{10} = \dfrac{12}{} = \dfrac{}{20} = \dfrac{}{} = \dfrac{}{30}$

d $\quad\dfrac{3}{10} = \dfrac{}{} = \dfrac{}{30} = \dfrac{}{50} = \dfrac{18}{}$

3 Copy and complete each of these statements.

a $\quad\dfrac{6}{8} = \dfrac{6 \div 2}{8 \div 2} = \dfrac{}{}$

b $\quad\dfrac{9}{12} = \dfrac{9 \div 3}{12 \div 3} = \dfrac{}{}$

c $\quad\dfrac{15}{25} = \dfrac{15 \div 5}{25 \div} = \dfrac{}{}$

d $\quad\dfrac{20}{70} = \dfrac{20 \div 10}{70 \div} = \dfrac{}{}$

4 Cancel down each of these fractions into their simplest form.

a $\frac{4}{10}$ b $\frac{3}{12}$ c $\frac{5}{25}$ d $\frac{6}{15}$ e $\frac{8}{12}$

f $\frac{10}{30}$ g $\frac{12}{20}$ h $\frac{16}{24}$ i $\frac{30}{50}$ j $\frac{42}{49}$

5 Put the following fractions in order with the smallest first.

a $\frac{1}{3}, \frac{1}{2}, \frac{1}{4}$ b $\frac{3}{4}, \frac{3}{8}, \frac{1}{2}$ c $\frac{5}{6}, \frac{2}{3}, \frac{7}{12}$ d $\frac{2}{5}, \frac{3}{10}, \frac{1}{4}$

HOMEWORK 2E

1 Change each of these top-heavy fractions into a mixed number.

a $\frac{5}{2}$ b $\frac{5}{3}$ c $\frac{7}{4}$ d $\frac{11}{3}$ e $\frac{9}{2}$ f $\frac{13}{4}$

g $\frac{11}{5}$ h $\frac{10}{4}$ i $\frac{14}{6}$ j $\frac{17}{8}$ k $\frac{17}{10}$ l $\frac{26}{8}$

m $\frac{12}{4}$ n $\frac{20}{5}$ o $\frac{60}{10}$

2 Change each of these mixed numbers into a top-heavy fraction.

a $1\frac{1}{2}$ b $2\frac{1}{4}$ c $2\frac{1}{3}$ d $4\frac{1}{2}$ e $3\frac{2}{3}$ f $1\frac{3}{4}$

g $2\frac{1}{5}$ h $2\frac{3}{8}$ i $3\frac{2}{5}$ j $4\frac{3}{5}$ k $5\frac{3}{8}$ l $4\frac{3}{7}$

m $5\frac{4}{9}$ n $4\frac{5}{12}$ o $7\frac{7}{10}$

HOMEWORK 2F

Example 1 $\frac{5}{9} + \frac{7}{9} = \frac{12}{9} = \frac{4}{3} = 1\frac{1}{3}$ (Cancel down and change to a mixed number.)

Example 2 $\frac{2}{3} + \frac{1}{5} = \frac{10}{15} + \frac{3}{15} = \frac{13}{15}$ (Use equivalent fractions to make the denominators the same.)

1 Calculate each of these additions. Remember to cancel down.

a $\frac{3}{8} + \frac{1}{8}$ b $\frac{3}{10} + \frac{5}{10}$ c $\frac{5}{12} + \frac{1}{12}$ d $\frac{1}{9} + \frac{5}{9}$ e $\frac{2}{15} + \frac{7}{15}$

2 Calculate each of these additions. Remember to change into mixed numbers.

a $\frac{5}{8} + \frac{7}{8}$ b $\frac{3}{4} + \frac{3}{4}$ c $\frac{7}{10} + \frac{3}{10}$ d $\frac{5}{12} + \frac{11}{12}$ e $\frac{13}{20} + \frac{11}{20}$

3 Calculate each of these additions. Remember to use equivalent fractions.

a $\frac{1}{3} + \frac{1}{2}$ b $\frac{2}{5} + \frac{3}{10}$ c $\frac{1}{4} + \frac{5}{12}$ d $\frac{3}{5} + \frac{1}{4}$

e $\frac{3}{4} + \frac{2}{3}$ f $\frac{5}{6} + \frac{1}{2}$ g $1\frac{1}{2} + 2\frac{1}{4}$ h $1\frac{1}{3} + 2\frac{3}{4}$

4 Calculate each of these subtractions.

a $\frac{5}{8} - \frac{1}{8}$ b $\frac{7}{10} - \frac{3}{10}$ c $\frac{11}{12} - \frac{3}{4}$ d $\frac{2}{3} - \frac{1}{2}$

e $\frac{9}{10} - \frac{1}{5}$ f $1 - \frac{3}{5}$ g $3 - 1\frac{1}{4}$ h $4\frac{3}{4} - 1\frac{1}{3}$

1   At a cricket match, $\frac{9}{10}$ of the crowd were men. What fraction of the crowd were women?

2   An iceberg shows $\frac{1}{9}$ of its mass above sea level. What fraction of it is below sea level?

3   A petrol gauge shows that a tank is $\frac{7}{12}$ full. What fraction of the tank is empty?

4   David spends $\frac{1}{4}$ of his pocket money on bus fares, $\frac{1}{3}$ on magazines and saves the rest. What fraction of his money does he save?

★5   In a local election Mr Weeks received $\frac{2}{5}$ of the total votes, Ms Meenan received $\frac{1}{4}$ and Mr White received the remainder. What fraction of the total votes did Mr White receive?

★6   On a certain day at a busy railway station, $\frac{7}{10}$ of the trains arriving were on time, $\frac{1}{6}$ were late by 10 minutes or less and the rest were late by more than 10 minutes. What fraction of the trains arrived late by more than 10 minutes?

1   Calculate each of these.
   a $\frac{1}{2} \times 20$ **b** $\frac{1}{3} \times 36$ **c** $\frac{1}{4} \times 24$ **d** $\frac{3}{4} \times 40$
   e $\frac{2}{3} \times 15$ **f** $\frac{1}{5} \times 30$ **g** $\frac{3}{8} \times 16$ **h** $\frac{7}{10} \times 50$

2   Calculate each of these quantities.
   a $\frac{1}{4}$ of £800   **b** $\frac{2}{3}$ of 60 kilograms   **c** $\frac{3}{4}$ of 200 metres
   d $\frac{3}{8}$ of 48 gallons   **e** $\frac{4}{5}$ of 30 minutes   **f** $\frac{7}{10}$ of 120 miles

3   In each case, find out which is the smaller number.
   a $\frac{1}{4}$ of 60 or $\frac{1}{2}$ of 40   **b** $\frac{1}{3}$ of 36 or $\frac{1}{5}$ of 50
   c $\frac{2}{3}$ of 15 or $\frac{3}{4}$ of 12   **d** $\frac{5}{8}$ of 72 or $\frac{5}{6}$ of 60

4 $\frac{5}{9}$ of a class of 36 students are girls. How many boys are there in the class?

5   Mrs Wilson puts $\frac{3}{20}$ of her weekly wage into a pension scheme. How much does she put into the scheme if her wage one week is £320?

6   Mitchell spent one third of a day sleeping and one quarter at school. How many hours are left for doing other things?

★7   A bush is 40 cm tall when planted in spring. Its height increases by $\frac{3}{10}$ during the summer.
   a   Find $\frac{3}{10}$ of 40 cm.
   b   Find the height of the bush at the end of the summer.

★8   A travel agent has this sign in their window. Marion books a holiday for her family which would normally cost £800.

⅕ OFF **all holiday prices for next year** **if booked before December**

   a   How much does she save?
   b   How much does she pay for the holiday after the reduction?

Example   Write £5 as a fraction of £20.

$\frac{5}{20} = \frac{1}{4}$ (Cancel down)

1   Write the first quantity as a fraction of the second.
   a   £2, £8   **b**   9 cm, 12 cm   **c**   18 miles, 30 miles
   d   200 g, 350 g   **e**   20 seconds, 1 minute   **f**   25p, £2

2   During a one hour TV programme, 10 minutes were devoted to adverts. What fraction of the time was given to adverts?

3   On a 80 mile car journey, 50 miles were driven on a motorway. What fraction of the journey was not driven on a motorway?

4   In a class, 24 students were right-handed and 6 students were left-handed. What fraction of the class were
   a   right-handed   **b**   left-handed?

 HOMEWORK 2J

Example $\frac{2}{3} \times \frac{1}{4} = \frac{2}{12} = \frac{1}{6}$ Multiply numerators and denominators and cancel if possible.

Work out each of these multiplications.
   1 $\frac{1}{2} \times \frac{1}{2}$ **2** $\frac{1}{3} \times \frac{1}{5}$ **3** $\frac{1}{4} \times \frac{1}{3}$ **4** $\frac{3}{4} \times \frac{1}{2}$ **5** $\frac{1}{3} \times \frac{3}{5}$
   6 $\frac{2}{3} \times \frac{1}{2}$ **7** $\frac{4}{5} \times \frac{1}{2}$ **8** $\frac{5}{6} \times \frac{1}{5}$ **9** $\frac{3}{8} \times \frac{2}{3}$ **10** $\frac{3}{10} \times \frac{5}{6}$

Chapter 3   Negative numbers

 HOMEWORK 3A

Copy and complete each of the following.

1   If +£20 means a profit of twenty pounds, then .... means a loss of twenty pounds.

2   If –£10 means a loss of ten pounds, then +£10 means a .... of ten pounds.

3   If +500 m means 500 metres above sea level, then .... means 500 metres below sea level.

4   If –1000 m means one thousand metres below sea level, then +1000 m means one thousand metres .... sea level.

5   If +7 °C means seven degrees above freezing point, then .... means seven degrees below freezing point.

6   If +1 °C means 1 °C above freezing point, then .... means 1 °C below freezing point.

7   If –15 °C means fifteen degrees below freezing point, then +15 °C means fifteen degrees .... freezing point.

8 If –5000 m means five thousand miles south of the equator, then +5000 m means five thousand miles .... of the equator.

9 If a car moving forwards at 25 mph is represented by +25 mph, then a car moving backwards at 10 mph is represented by ....

10 In multi-storey car park, the sixth floor above ground level is represented by +6. So, the third floor below ground level is represented by ....

HOMEWORK 3B

Use the number line to answer questions 1 and 2.

-7 -6 -5 -4 -3 -2 -1 0 1 2 3 4 5 6 7

Negative   **Positive**

1 Complete each of the foliowing by putting a suitable number in the box.
   a ☐ is smaller than 6   b ☐ is smaller than 2
   c ☐ is smaller than –1   d ☐ is smaller than –6
   e –4 is smaller than ☐   f –7 is smaller than ☐
   g 5 is smaller than ☐   h 4 is smaller than ☐
   i ☐ is smaller than 0   j –1 is smaller than ☐

2 Complete each of the following by putting a suitable number in the box.
   a ☐ is bigger than –6   b ☐ is bigger than 4
   c ☐ is bigger than –2   d ☐ is bigger than 0
   e –3 is bigger than ☐   f –5 is bigger than ☐
   g 1 is bigger than ☐   h –1 is bigger than ☐
   i ☐ is bigger than –4   j 3 is bigger than ☐

3 In each case below, put the correct symbol, either < or >, in the box.
   Reminder: The inequality signs: < means 'is less than' and > means 'is greater than'.
   a 2 ☐ 6   b –1 ☐ –7   c –5 ☐ 1   d 5 ☐ 9
   e –8 ☐ 2   f –14 ☐ –10   g –11 ☐ 0   h –9 ☐ –12
   i 8 ☐ –3   j 0 ☐ –8

4 Copy these number lines and fill in the missing numbers on each line.
   a
      –10   –2   0   2   10

   b
         –20   –10   0   10   20

   c
            –20   0   20

   d
               –100   0   200

   e
         –100   0   100

Example 1 $-3 + 5 = 2$

Example 2 $-4 - 5 = -9$

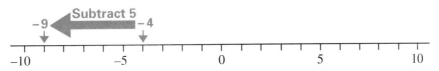

1 Use the number line to find the answer to each of the following.

a	$-2 + 5 =$	**b**	$-4 + 6 =$	**c**	$-3 + 4 =$	**d**	$-1 + 5 =$
e	$-6 + 8 =$	**f**	$-5 + 10 =$	**g**	$-2 + 2 =$	**h**	$-4 + 4 =$
i	$4 - 5 =$	**j**	$6 - 8 =$	**k**	$3 - 7 =$	**l**	$5 - 9 =$
m	$-5 + 3 =$	**n**	$-2 + 1 =$	**o**	$-10 + 6 =$	**p**	$-8 + 6 =$
q	$-2 - 7 =$	**r**	$-1 - 5 =$	**s**	$-3 - 7 =$	**t**	$-5 - 5 =$

2 Answer each of the following without the help of the number scale.

a	$15 - 19 =$	**b**	$3 - 17 =$	**c**	$-2 - 10 =$	**d**	$-12 + 7 =$
e	$-15 + 9 =$	**f**	$10 - 20 =$	**g**	$-10 - 12 =$	**h**	$-15 - 20 =$
i	$23 - 30 =$						

3 Work out each of the following.

a	$1 + 3 - 5 =$	**b**	$-4 + 8 - 2 =$	**c**	$-6 + 3 - 4 =$	**d**	$-3 - 5 + 4 =$
e	$-1 - 1 + 5 =$	**f**	$-7 + 5 + 8 =$	**g**	$-3 - 4 + 7 =$	**h**	$1 - 3 - 6 =$
i	$-5 - 3 - 2 =$						

Example 1 $4 - (-2) = 4 + 2 = 6$

Example 2 $3 + (-5) = 3 - 5 = -2$

1 Answer each of the following. Check your answers on a calculator.

a	$2 + (-5) =$	**b**	$6 - (-3) =$	**c**	$3 + (-5) =$	**d**	$8 - (-2) =$
e	$-6 + (-2) =$	**f**	$-5 + (-2) =$	**g**	$-2 - (-5) =$	**h**	$-7 - (-1) =$
i	$-2 - (-2) =$						

2 Write down the answer to each of the following, then check your answers on a calculator.

a	$-13 - 5 =$	**b**	$-12 - 8 =$	**c**	$-25 + 6 =$	**d**	$6 - 14 =$
e	$25 - -3 =$	**f**	$13 - -8 =$	**g**	$-4 + -15 =$	**h**	$-13 + -7 =$
i	$-12 + -9 =$	**j**	$-16 + -12 =$				

3 The temperature at midday was 5 °C. Find the temperature at midnight if it fell by:

a	1 °C	**b**	5 °C	**c**	6 °C	**d**	8 °C	**e**	12 °C

4 What is the difference between the following temperatures?

a	4 °C and 6 °C	**b**	−2 °C and 4 °C	**c**	−3 °C and −6 °C

5 Rewrite the following lists, putting the numbers in order of size, smallest first.

  a   2   −5   3   −6   −3   8   −1   1

  b   4   −8   5   −10   −5   0   6   −12

★6 You have the following cards.

  a   Which other card should you choose to make the answer to the following sum as large as possible? What is the answer?

  b   Which other card should you choose to make the answer to part **a** as small as possible? What is the answer?

  c   Which other card should you choose to make the answer to the following sum as large as possible? What is the answer?

  d   Which other card should you choose to make the answer to part **c** as small as possible? What is the answer?

  e   Which two cards should you choose to make the answer to an addition sum zero?

HOMEWORK 3E

1 Find the next three numbers in each sequence.

  a   6, 4, 2, 0, …, …, …   **b**   8, 5, 2, −1, …, …, …

  c   −20, −15, −10, −5, …, …, …   **d**   10, 9, 7, 4, …, …, …

  e $-12, -10\frac{1}{2}, -9, -7\frac{1}{2}, …, …, …$

2 The deep freeze compartment in a refrigerator should be set at −14 °C, but in error is set to −6 °C. What is the difference between the two settings?

3 At 5am, the temperature on a thermometer outside Brian's house was −4 °C. By midday, the temperature had risen by 10 °C.

  a   What was the temperature at midday?

  By midnight, the temperature had fallen to −9 °C.

  b   What was the fall in temperature from midday to midnight?

★4 The table shows the recorded highest and lowest temperatures in five cities during one year.

	London	New York	Athens	Beijing	Nairobi
Highest temperature (°C)	30	28	36	31	29
Lowest temperature (°C)	−5	−8	5	−10	11

  a   Which city had the highest temperature?

  b   Which city had the largest difference in temperature and by how many degrees?

  c   Which city had the smallest difference in temperature and by how many degrees?

★5 This is a two step function machine. Use the function machine to complete the table.

| Number in | ⮕ | Add 2 | ⮕ | Subtract 5 | ⮕ | Number out |

Number in	Number out
10	
2	
−1	
	0
	−8

Chapter 4   More about number

HOMEWORK 4A

1 Write out the first five multiples of:
   a   4   **b**   6   **c**   8   **d**   12   **e**   15
   Remember: the first multiple is the number itself.

2 From the list of numbers below
   28   19   36   43   64   53   77   66   56   60   15   29   61   45   51
   write down those that are:
   a   multiples of 4   **b**   multiples of 5   **c**   multiples of 8   **d**   multiples of 11

3 Use your calculator to see which of the numbers below are
   a   multiples of 7   **b**   multiples of 9   **c**   multiples of 12
   225   252   361   297   162   363   161   289   224   205   312   378   315   182   369

4 Find the biggest number smaller than 200 that is
   a   a multiple of 2   **b**   a multiple of 4   **c**   a multiple of 5   **d**   a multiple of 8
   e   a multiple of 9

5 Find the smallest number that is a multiple of 3 and bigger than
   a   10   **b**   100   **c**   1000   **d**   10 000   **e**   1 000 000 000

HOMEWORK 4B

Example   Find the factors of 32

Look for the pairs of numbers which make 32 when multiplied together. These are
$1 \times 32 = 32$ $2 \times 16 = 32$ $4 \times 8 = 32$ So the factors of 32 are 1, 2, 4, 8, 16, 32.

1 What are the factors of each of these numbers?
   a   12   **b**   13   **c**   15   **d**   20   **e**   22
   f   36   **g**   42   **h**   48   **i**   49   **j**   50

2 Use your calculator to find the factors of each of these numbers.
   a   100   **b**   111   **c**   125   **d**   132   **e**   140

3 All the numbers are divisible by 11. Use your calculator to divide each one by 11 and then write down the answer. What do you notice?

a 143	**b** 253	**c** 275	**d** 363	**e** 462
f 484	**g** 561	**h** 583	**i** 792	**j** 891

HOMEWORK 4C

1 Write down all the prime numbers less than 40.

2 Which of these numbers are prime?

43   47   49   51   54   57   59   61   65   67

3 This is a number pattern to generate odd numbers.

Line 1 $2 - 1 = 1$
Line 2 $2 \times 2 - 1 = 3$
Line 3 $2 \times 2 \times 2 - 1 = 7$

a Work out the next three lines of the pattern.

b Which lines have answers that are prime numbers?

4 Write down the first ten square numbers.

5 Here is another number pattern.

$2 \times 0 + 1 = 1$
$3 \times 1 + 1 = 4$
$4 \times 2 + 1 = 9$

a Write down the next three lines in the pattern.

b Describe what you notice about the answers to each line of the pattern.

6 Write down the answer to each of the following. You will need to use your calculator.

a 5^2	**b** 15^2	**c** 25^2	**d** 35^2	**e** 45^2
f 55^2	**g** 65^2	**h** 75^2	**i** 85^2	**j** 95^2

Describe any pattern you notice.

HOMEWORK 4D

1 Write down the square root of each of these.

a 64	**b** 25	**c** 49	**d** 81	**e** 16
f 36	**g** 100	**h** 121	**i** 144	**j** 400

2 Write down the answer to each of the following. You will need to use your calculator.

a $\sqrt{225}$	**b** $\sqrt{289}$	**c** $\sqrt{441}$	**d** $\sqrt{625}$	**e** $\sqrt{1089}$
f $\sqrt{1369}$	**g** $\sqrt{3136}$	**h** $\sqrt{6084}$	**i** $\sqrt{40\,804}$	**j** $\sqrt{110\,889}$

3 A number pattern using square roots and square numbers.

$\sqrt{1} = 1$
$\sqrt{1} + \sqrt{4} = 3$
$\sqrt{1} + \sqrt{4} + \sqrt{9} = 6$

a Write down the next three lines in the pattern.

b Describe any pattern you notice in the answers.

Example   Work out 3^5

$$3^5 = 3 \times 3 \times 3 \times 3 \times 3 = 243$$

1 Use your calculator to work out the value of each of the following.

    a 2^3 **b** 4^3 **c** 7^3 **d** 10^3 **e** 12^3

    f 3^4 **g** 10^4 **h** 2^5 **i** 10^6 **j** 2^8

2 Use your calculator to work out the answers to the following powers of 11.

    a 11^2 **b** 11^3 **c** 11^4

    Describe any patterns you notice in your answers.

    Does your pattern work for other powers of 11? Give a reason for your answer.

★3

1	2	3	4	5	6	7	8	9
10	11	12	13	14	15	16	17	18
19	20	21	22	23	24	25	26	27
28	29	30	31	32	33	34	35	36

From the numbers above, write down

    a all the multiples of 7   **b** all the factors of 30

    c all the prime numbers   **d** the square of 6

    e the square root of 25   **f** the cube of 3

Chapter 5 Some plane shapes

1 Calculate the perimeter of each of the following shapes.

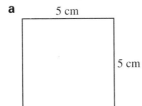

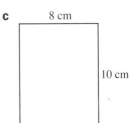

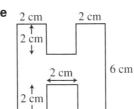
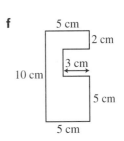

2 Draw as many different rectangles as possible with a perimeter of 14 cm.

3 Is it possible to draw a rectangle with a perimeter of 9 cm? Explain your answer.

1 By counting squares, find the area of each of these shapes.

a

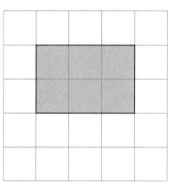

b

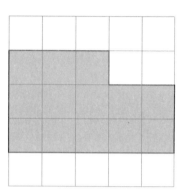

c

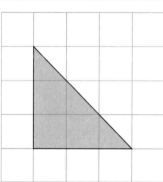

d

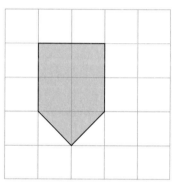

2 By counting squares, estimate the area of each of these shapes.

a

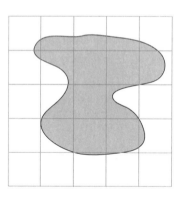

b

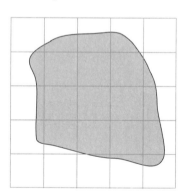

c

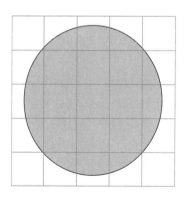

d

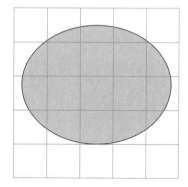

1 Calculate the area and the perimeter of each rectangle below.

a 5 cm, 2 cm

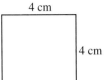

b 4 cm, 4 cm

c 2 m, 8 m

d 12 mm, 3 mm

e 20 m, 10 m

2 Copy and complete the following table for rectangles **a** to **e**.

	Length	Width	Perimeter	Area
a	4 cm	2 cm		
b	7 cm	4 cm		
c	6 cm		22 cm	
d		3 cm		15 cm²
e			30 cm	50 cm²

3 Copy and complete:

a $1 \text{ cm}^2 = \ldots\ldots \text{ mm}^2$ **b** $1 \text{ m}^2 = \ldots\ldots \text{ cm}^2$

Calculate the area of each shape below as follows.
- First, split it into rectangles.
- Then, calculate the area of each rectangle.
- Finally, add together the areas of the rectangles.

1

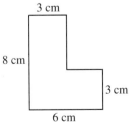

3 cm, 8 cm, 3 cm, 6 cm

2

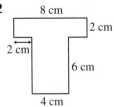

8 cm, 2 cm, 2 cm, 6 cm, 4 cm

3

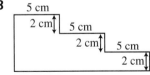

5 cm, 2 cm, 5 cm, 2 cm, 5 cm, 2 cm

4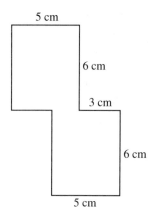

5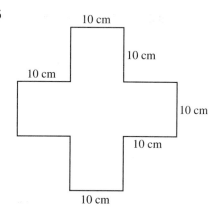

HOMEWORK 5E

Example Find the area of this triangle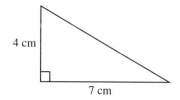

$$\text{Area} = \tfrac{1}{2} \times 7 \times 4$$
$$= \tfrac{1}{2} \times 28 = 14 \, \text{cm}^2$$

1 Write down the perimeter and area of each triangle.

a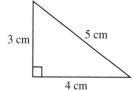

b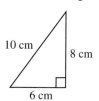

c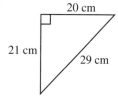

2 Find the areas of these composite shapes.

a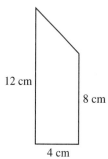

b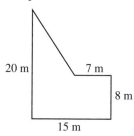

c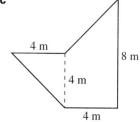

★**3** Find the area of the wood on this blackboard 90° set-square.

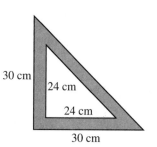

★4 Which of these three triangles has the smallest area?

a
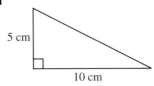
5 cm
10 cm

b
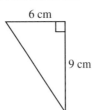
6 cm
9 cm

c

12 cm
4 cm

HOMEWORK 5F

Example   Find the area of this triangle.

$$\text{Area} = \tfrac{1}{2} \times 9 \times 4$$
$$= \tfrac{1}{2} \times 36 = 18\,\text{cm}^2$$

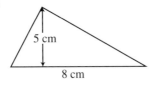
4 cm
9 cm

1   Calculate the area of each of these triangles.

a
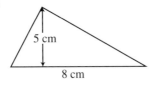
5 cm
8 cm

b
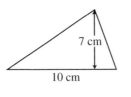
7 cm
10 cm

c
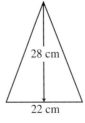
28 cm
22 cm

d
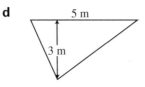
5 m
3 m

e
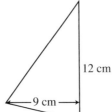
12 cm
9 cm

f
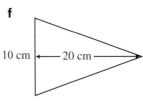
10 cm   20 cm

2   Copy and complete the following table for triangles **a** to **e**.

	Base	Vertical height	Area
a	6 cm	8 cm	
b	10 cm	7 cm	
c	5 cm	5 cm	
d	4 cm		12 cm²
e		20 cm	50 cm²

★3 Find the area of each of the shaded shapes.

a
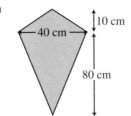
40 cm
10 cm
80 cm

b
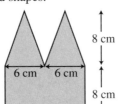
8 cm
6 cm   6 cm
8 cm

c
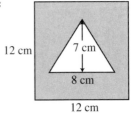
12 cm
7 cm
8 cm
12 cm

★4 Draw diagrams to show two different-sized triangles that have the same area of 40 cm².

Example   Find the area of this parallelogram.

$$\text{Area} = 8 \times 6$$
$$= 48\,\text{cm}^2$$

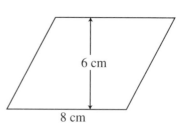

1   Calculate the area of each parallelogram below.

a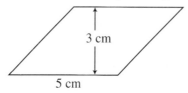

b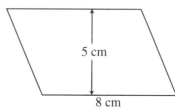

c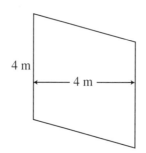

d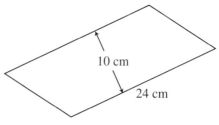

2   Find the area of the shaded shape.

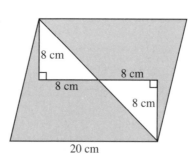

Chapter 6   Some statistics

1   For the following surveys, decide whether the data should be collected by:
   i sampling   **ii** observation   **iii** experiment
   a   The number of 'doubles' obtained when throwing two dice.
   b   The number of people who use a zebra-crossing on a busy main road.
   c   People's choice of favourite restaurant.
   d   The makes of cars parked on the staff car-park.
   e   The number of times a 'head' appears when throwing a coin.
   f   The type of food students prefer to eat in the school canteen.

2 In a game, a fair six-sided dice has its faces numbered 0, 1 or 2.

The dice is thrown 36 times and the results are as follows:

2 0 2 2 1 2 0 2 2 0 0 2
1 2 2 2 0 2 2 0 1 2 2 1
0 2 2 0 2 0 2 2 0 1 2 0

a Copy and complete the frequency table for the data.

Number	Tally	Frequency
0		
1		
2		

b Based on the results in the table, how many times do you think each number appears on the dice?

★**3** The table shows the average daily highest temperature recorded during August in 24 cities around the world.

City	Temperature (°C)	City	Temperature (°C)
Athens	33	Madras	35
Auckland	15	Marrakesh	38
Bangkok	32	Moscow	22
Budapest	27	Narvik	16
Buenos Aires	16	Nice	29
Cape Town	18	Oporto	25
Dubai	39	Perth	17
Geneva	25	Pisa	30
Istanbul	28	Quebec	23
La Paz	17	Reykjavik	14
London	20	Tokyo	30
Luxor	41	Tripoli	31

a Copy and complete the grouped frequency table for the data.

Temperature (°C)	Tally	Frequency
11–15		
16–20		
21–25		
26–30		
31–35		
36–40		
41– 45		

b In how many cities was the temperature higher than the temperature in London?

c Kay said that the difference between the highest and lowest temperatures was 34 °C but Derek said that it is was 27 °C. Explain how they obtained different answers.

★**4** Heather attends a Spanish evening class at her local college. One evening she conducted a survey of the ages of all the people who attended. She wrote down all the ages on a piece of paper as follows.

```
25  41  33  24  46
   37  40  32  59
64  37   26  44
 58  31   29  19
 37  30  22
  48  51   68  28  27
        51  34  49
```

a How many people attended on that evening?

b Copy and complete the grouped frequency table for the data.

Age	Tally	Frequency
11–20		
21–30		
31–40		
41–50		
51–60		
61–70		

c How many people were aged under 21? Give a reason for your answer.

5 Pat measured the heights, to the nearest centimetre, of all the students in her class. Her data is given below.

143 135 147 153 146 138 151
142 139 131 144 127 143 145
140 143 153 141 150 137 136
125 136 140 131 147 154 142

a Draw a grouped frequency table for the data using class intervals 125–129, 130–134, 135–139 …

b In which interval do the most heights lie?

c How many students had a height of 140 cm or more?

HOMEWORK 6B

1 The pictogram shows the number of copies of *The Times* sold by a newsagent in a particular week.

		Total
Monday	▬ ▬ ▬	12
Tuesday	▬ ▬ ▬ ▬	
Wednesday	▬ ▬ ▪	
Thursday	▬ ▬ ▬ ▬	
Friday		
Saturday		

a How many newspapers does the symbol ▬ represent?

b Complete the totals for Tuesday, Wednesday and Thursday.

c The newsagent sold 15 copies on Friday and 22 copies on Saturday.
Complete the pictogram for Friday and Saturday.

2 The pictogram shows the amount of sunshine in five English holiday resorts on one day in August.

Blackpool	Brighton	Scarborough	Skegness	Torbay
✸✸✸	✸◖	✸✸✸	✸✸	✸✸✸◖

Key. ✸ represents 3 hours.

a Write down the number of hours of sunshine for each resort.

b Great Yarmouth had $5\frac{1}{2}$ hours of sunshine on the same day. Explain why this would be difficult to show on this pictogram.

★**3** The pictogram shows the number of call-outs five taxi drivers had on one evening.

Brian ✪ ✪

Mike ✪ ✪

Robert ✪ ◖

Steve ✪ ✪ ◖

Terry ✪ ◖

Key. ✪ represents 10 call-outs.

a How many call-outs did each taxi driver have?

b Explain why the symbol used in this pictogram is not really suitable.

c Joanne had 16 call-outs on the same evening. Redraw a suitable pictogram to show the call-outs for the six taxi drivers.

4 Rachel did a survey to show the number of people in each car on their way to work on a particular morning. This is a copy of her survey sheet.

No of people in each car	Frequency
1	30
2	19
3	12
4	5
5 or more	1

Draw a pictogram to illustrate her data.

1 Linda asked a sample of people 'What is your favourite soap opera?' The bar chart shows their replies.

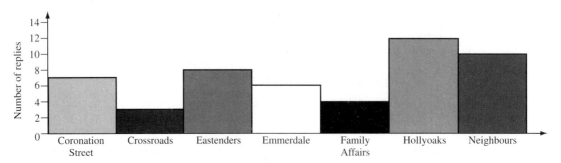

a Which soap opera got 6 replies?

b How many people were in Linda's sample?

c Linda collected the data from all her friends in Year 10 at school. Give two reasons why this is not a good way to collect the data.

2 The bar chart shows the results of a survey of shoe sizes in form 10KE.

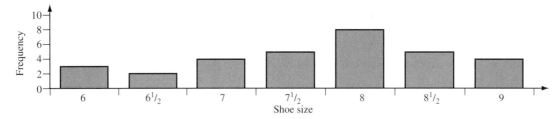

a How many students wear size $7\frac{1}{2}$ shoes?

b How many students were in the survey?

c What is the most common shoe size?

d Can you tell how many boys were in the survey? Explain your answer.

3 The table shows the lowest and highest marks six students got in a series of mental arithmetic tests.

	Abigail	Ben	Chris	Dave	Emma	Fay
Lowest mark	7	11	10	10	15	9
Highest mark	11	12	12	13	16	14

Draw a dual bar chart to illustrate the data.

4 The following data shows the times, to the nearest minute, how long patients had to wait before seeing a doctor.

    5   12   14   24   32   7   12   35   23   27   13   6
   28   4   20   13   40   5   2   11   16   31   10   26
   25   30   29   9   12   27   13   20   24   11   14   38

a Draw a grouped frequency table to show the waiting times of the patients, using class intervals 1–10, 11–20 , 21–30, 31–40.

b Draw a bar chart to illustrate the data.

5 Richard did a survey to find out which brand of crisps his friends preferred.
He drew this bar chart to illustrate his data.

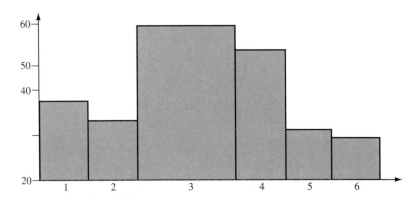

Richard's bar chart is very misleading. Explain how he could improve it and then redraw it, taking into account all your improvements.

HOMEWORK 6D

1 The line graph shows the monthly average exchange rate of the Spanish Peseta for £1 over a six month period.

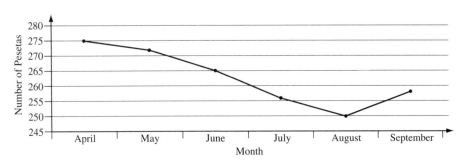

   a In which month was the lowest exchange rate and what was that value?
   b By how much did the exchange rate fall from April to August?
   c Which month had the greatest fall in the exchange rate from the previous month?
   d Mr Hargreaves changed £200 into pesetas during July. How many pesetas did he receive?

★2 The table shows the temperature in Cuzco in Peru over a 24 hour period.

Time	0000	0400	0800	1200	1600	2000	2400
Temperature (°C)	1	−4	6	15	21	9	−1

   a Draw a line graph for the data.
   b From your graph estimate the temperature at 1800.

★3 The table shows the value, to the nearest million pounds, of a country's imports and exports.

Year	1995	1996	1997	1998	1999	2000
Imports	22	35	48	51	62	55
Exports	35	41	56	53	63	58

   a Draw line graphs on the same axes to show the imports and exports of the country.
   b Find the smallest and greatest difference between the imports and exports.

HOMEWORK 7A

1 Write down the algebraic expression that says
   a   4 more than x **b**   7 less than x **c** k more than 3
   d t less than 8   **e** x added to y **f** x multiplied by 4
   g   5 multiplied by t **h** a multiplied by b **i** m divided by 2
   j p divided by q

2 Val is x years old. Dave is four years older than Val and Ella is five years younger than Val.
   a   How old is Dave?   **b**   How old is Ella?

3 A packet contains n sweets.

The total number of sweets here
is $2n + 3$.
Write down an expression for the total number of sweets in the following.
   a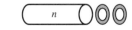

   b

   c

4 Sue has p pets.
   ●   Frank has two more pets than Sue.
   ●   Chloe has three less pets than Sue.
   ●   Lizzie has twice as many pets as Sue.
   How many pets does each person have?

5   **a**   Tom has £20 and spends £16. How much does he have left?
   b   Sam has £10 and spends £a. How much does he have left?
   c   Ian has £b and spends £c. How much does he have left?

6   **a**   How many days are there in 3 weeks?
   b   How many days are there in z weeks?

★7   **a**   Granny Parker divides £30 equally between her 3 grand-children. How much does
     each receive?
   b   Granny Smith divides £r equally between her 4 grand-children How much does each
     receive?
   c   Granny Thomas divides £p equally between her q grand-children. How much does
     each receive?

HOMEWORK 7B

Example 1 $x + 3x + 2x - 4x = 2x$

Example 2 $2a + 3b + 5a + 2b - 4a - b = 3a + 4b$

Example 3 $3(2t - 5) = 6t - 15$

Example 4 $x(x + 2) = x^2 + 2x$

Example 5   Factorise the following

   a $10t + 15 = 5(2t + 3)$
   b $x^2 - 3x = x(x - 3)$

1   Write each of these expressions in a shorter form.
   a $a + a + a$
   b $3b + 2b$
   c $3c + c + 5c$
   d $5d - d$
   e $5e + 2e - 4e$
   f $7f - 2f + 3f$
   g $2g + 4g - 6g$
   h $4h - 6h$
   i $3i^2 + 2i^2$
   j $5j^2 + j^2 - 2j^2$

2   Simplify each of the following expressions.
   a $2y + 5x + y + 3x$
   b $4m + 6p - 2m + 4p$
   c $3x + 6 + 3x - 2$
   d $7 - 5x - 2 + 8x$
   e $5p + 2t + 3p - 2t$
   f $4 + 2x + 4x - 6$
   g $4p - 4 - 2p - 2$
   h $4x + 3y + 2x - 5y$
   i $4 + 3t + p - 6t + 3 + 5p$
   j $4w - 3k - 2w - k + 4w$

3   Multiply out each of the following brackets.
   a $2(a + 4)$
   b $3(b - 3)$
   c $5(c + 1)$
   d $2(2e + 5)$
   e $4(3e - 1)$
   f $5(5m + 7)$
   g $2(5a + 2b)$
   h $2(3x - 4y)$
   i $3(4p + q)$
   j $a(a + 3)$
   k $b(b - 2)$
   l $x(2x + 5)$

4   Factorise each of these.
   a $3a + 9$
   b $5b + 25$
   c $6c + 4$
   d $8d - 6$
   e $10e - 15$
   f $5f - 5$
   g $8g - 12$
   h $5 + 10h$
   i $21 - 14i$
   j $x^2 + 5x$
   k $y^2 + 4y$
   l $z^2 - z$

HOMEWORK 7C

Example   The expression $3x + 2$ has the value 5 when $x = 1$ and 14 when $x = 4$

1   Find the value of $2x + 3$ when
   a $x = 2$
   b $x = 5$
   c $x = 10$

2   Find the value of $3k - 4$ when
   a $k = 2$
   b $k = 6$
   c $k = 12$

3   Find the value of $4 + t$ when
   a $t = 4$
   b $t = 20$
   c $t = \frac{1}{2}$

4   Evaluate $10 - 2x$ when
   a $x = 3$
   b $x = 5$
   c $x = 6$

5   Evaluate $5y + 10$ when
   a $y = 5$
   b $y = 10$
   c $y = 15$

6   Evaluate $6d - 2$ when
   a $d = 2$
   b $d = 5$
   c $d = \frac{1}{2}$

7   Find the value of $\frac{x + 2}{4}$ when
   a $x = 6$
   b $x = 10$
   c $x = 18$

8 Find the value of $\dfrac{3x-1}{2}$ when

    a $x=1$ **b** $x=3$ **c** $x=4$

9 Evaluate $\dfrac{20}{p}$ when

    a $p=2$ **b** $p=10$ **c** $p=20$

10 Find the value of $3(2y+5)$ when

    a $y=1$ **b** $y=3$ **c** $y=5$

HOMEWORK 7D

Example   The formula for the perimeter of a rectangle is $P = 2a + 2b$. Find P when $a = 5$ and $b = 3$.

$$P = 2 \times 5 + 2 \times 3 = 10 + 6 = 16$$

1 For $A = t + h$, find A when

    a $t=2$ and $h=3$ **b** $t=4$ and $h=7$ **c** $t=10$ and $h=19$

2 For $P = 2x - 4y$, find P when

    a $x=5$ and $y=2$ **b** $x=6$ and $y=1$ **c** $x=8$ and $y=4$

3 For $a = 3b + 5c$, find a when

    a $b=2$ and $c=3$ **b** $b=3$ and $c=5$ **c** $b=2$ and c $=-2$

4 For $e = f^2 + g^2$, find e when

    a $f=2$ and $g=3$ **b** $f=3$ and $g=4$ **c** $f=5$ and $g=10$

5 For $y = \sqrt{x} + n$, find y when

    a $x=16$ and $n=5$ **b** $x=49$ and $n=3$ **c** $x=100$ and $n=50$

6 The formula to find the distance travelled in miles (d) is given by $d = st$ where s is the average speed in miles per hour and t is the time in hours. Find d when

    a $s=3$ and $t=2$ **b** $s=50$ and $t=4$ **c** $s=85$ and $t=6$

7 The formula $W = B + RT$ can be used to calculate a person's wage, where W is the total wage, B is the bonus, R is the rate of pay per hour and T is the number of hours worked. Find W when

    a $B=10$, $R=6$ and $T=7$ **b** $B=40$, $R=25$ and $T=40$

8 The formula for the area of a trapezium is given by $A = \dfrac{(a+b)h}{2}$

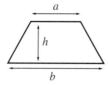

Find the area of a trapezium when

    a $a=3$, $b=4$ and $h=2$

    b $a=5$, $b=7$ and $h=10$

Chapter 8   Further number skills

HOMEWORK 8A

1 24×13	**2** 33×17	**3** 54×42	**4** 89×23	**5** 58×53
6 176×14	**7** 235×16	**8** 439×21	**9** 572×35	**10** 678×57

HOMEWORK 8B

1 $312 \div 13$	**2** $480 \div 15$	**3** $697 \div 17$	**4** $792 \div 22$	**5** $806 \div 26$
6 $532 \div 28$	**7** $736 \div 32$	**8** $595 \div 35$	**9** $948 \div 41$	**10** $950 \div 53$

HOMEWORK 8C

1 Wall tiles are packed in boxes of 16. Andy buys 24 packs to tile his bathroom. How many tiles does he buy altogether?

2 The organiser of a church fete requires 1000 coloured balloons. How many packets does she need to buy if there are 25 balloons in a packet?

3 A TV rental shop purchases 32 televisions at £112 each.
   a Find the total cost of the televisions.
   b Show how you could check your answer by estimation.

4 The annual subscription fee to join a Fishing Club is £42. The treasurer of the club has collected £1134 in fees. How many people have paid their subscription fee?

5 Mrs Woodhead saves £14 per week towards her bills. How much does she save in a year?

6 Sylvia has a part time job and is paid £18 for every day she works. Last year she worked for 148 days. How much was she paid for the year?

7 A coach firm charges £504 for 36 people to go Christmas shopping on a day trip to Calais. How much does each person pay if they share the cost equally between them?

8 A concert hall has 48 rows of seats with 32 seats in a row. What is the maximum capacity of the hall?

★9 Allan is a market gardener and has 420 bulbs to plant. He plants them out in rows with 18 bulbs to a row. How many complete rows will there be?

★10 A room measuring 6 metres by 8 metres is to be carpeted. The carpet costs £19 per square metre.
   a Estimate the cost of the carpet.
   b Calculate the exact cost of the carpet.

Examples.

5.852 will round off to 5.85 to two decimal places

7.156 will round off to 7.16 to two decimal places

0.284 will round off to 0.3 to one decimal place

15.3518 will round off to 15.4 to one decimal place

1 Round off each of the following numbers to one decimal place.

a 3.73 **b** 8.69 **c** 5.34 **d** 18.75 **e** 0.423

f 26.288 **g** 3.755 **h** 10.056 **i** 11.08 **j** 12.041

2 Round off each of the following numbers to two decimal places.

a 6.721 **b** 4.457 **c** 1.972 **d** 3.485 **e** 5.807

f 2.564 **g** 21.799 **h** 12.985 **i** 2.302 **j** 5.555

3 Round off each of the following to the number of decimal places indicated.

a 4.572 (1 dp) **b** 0.085 (2 dp) **c** 5.7159 (3 dp) **d** 4.558 (2 dp)

e 2.099 (2 dp) **f** 0.7629 (3 dp) **g** 7.124 (1 dp) **h** 8.903 (2 dp)

i 23.7809 (3 dp) **j** 0.99 (1 dp)

4 Round off each of the following to the nearest whole number.

a 6.7 **b** 9.3 **c** 2.8 **d** 7.5 **e** 8.38

f 2.82 **g** 2.18 **h** 1.55 **i** 5.252 **j** 3.999

Example Work out 4.2 + 8 + 12.93. Set out the sum as follows

Remember to keep the points in the same column.

$$
\begin{array}{r}
4.20 \\
8.00 \\
+ 12.93 \\
\hline
25.13 \\
\hline
{\scriptstyle 1\ 1}
\end{array}
$$

1 Work out each of these.

a 7.3 + 2.6 **b** 15.7 + 5.6 **c** 33.5 + 6.8 **d** 8.5 + 4.82

e 3.26 + 4.5 **f** 2.75 + 9.84 **g** 24.5 + 6.3 **h** 8.4 + 12.8

i 13.75 + 8.5 **j** 7.08 + 0.7 **k** 7 + 2.96 + 3.1 **l** 8.5 + 7.36 + 12.1

2 Work out each of these.

a 5.8 − 3.4 **b** 7.3 − 2.8 **c** 4.6 − 2.7 **d** 9.7 − 4.7

e 8.35 − 4.24 **f** 9.74 − 3.81 **g** 9.04 − 5.72 **h** 3.62 − 1.85

i 6 − 3.3 **j** 8 − 7.4 **k** 12 − 3.2 **l** 7.2 − 4.72

Example 1 $4.5 \times 3 =$

$$
\begin{array}{r}
4.5 \\
\times\ \ 3 \\
\hline
13.5 \\
\hline
{\scriptstyle 1}
\end{array}
$$

Example 2 $8.25 \div 5 =$

$$
\begin{array}{r}
1.6\ 5 \\
5\,\overline{)8.^{3}2^{2}5}
\end{array}
$$

Example 3   5.7 ÷ 2 = $\dfrac{2.\,8\,5}{2\,\overline{\vert\,5.^1 7^1 0}}$

1 Evaluate each of these.

    a 2.3×3 **b** 4.8×2 **c** 4.6×4 **d** 15.3×5 **e** 26.4×8

2 Evaluate each of these.

    a 2.14×2 **b** 3.45×3 **c** 5.47×6 **d** 4.44×8 **e** 0.25×9

3 Evaluate each of these.

    a $4.8 \div 2$ **b** $7.6 \div 4$ **c** $7.2 \div 3$ **d** $7.35 \div 5$ **e** $0.78 \div 6$

4 Evaluate each of these.

    a $4.5 \div 2$ **b** $7.2 \div 5$ **c** $3.4 \div 4$ **d** $13.1 \div 5$ **e** $6.3 \div 8$

★5 Crisps are sold in packs of six for £1.32 or packs of eight for £1.92. Which are the cheaper crisps?

★6 Steve took his wife and three children on a day trip by train to London. The tickets were £26.60 for each adult and £12.85 for each child. How much did the tickets cost Steve altogether?

 HOMEWORK 8G

Example   Evaluate 4.27 × 34 =

                                          4.27
                                 ×   34
                                  17.08 (multiply by 4)
                               128.10 (multiply by 3 and keep points in same column)
                               145.18

1 Evaluate each of these.

    a 3.12×14 **b** 5.24×15 **c** 1.36×22 **d** 7.53×25 **e** 27.1×32

2 Find the total cost of each of the following purchases.

    a Twenty-four litres of petrol at £0.78 per litre

    b Eighteen pints of milk at £0.28 per pint.

    c Fourteen magazines at £2.25 per copy.

3 The table shows the exchange rate for various currencies

Currency	Exchange rate
French franc (F)	£1 = 10.25F
American dollar ($)	£1 = $1.39
German mark (DM)	£1 = 3.06DM

    a Douglas changes £25 into francs. How many francs does he get?

    b Martin changes £32 into dollars. How many dollars does he get?

    c Pauline changes £45 into marks. How many marks does she get?

To multiply one decimal number by another decimal number:
● First, do the whole calculation as if the decimal points were not there.
● Then, count the total number of decimal places in the two decimal numbers. This gives the number of decimal places in the answer.

Example   Evaluate 3.42×0.2

Ignoring the decimal points gives the following calculation: $342 \times 2 = 684$

Now, 3.42 has 2 decimal places and 0.2 has 1 decimal place. So, the total number of decimal places in the answer is 3, which gives $3.42 \times 0.2 = 0.684$

1   Evaluate each of these.
   a 2.3×0.2 **b** 5.2×0.3 **c** 4.6×0.4 **d** 0.2×0.3 **e** 0.4×0.7
   f 0.5×0.5 **g** 12.6×0.6 **h** 7.2×0.7 **i** 1.4×1.2 **j** 2.6×1.5

2   For each of the following:
   i   Estimate the answer by first rounding off each number to the nearest whole number.
   ii   Calculate the exact answer, and then, by doing a subtraction, calculate how much out your answer to part **i** is.
   a 3.7×2.4 **b** 4.8×3.1 **c** 5.1×4.2 **d** 6.5×2.5

Example 1   Express 0.32 as a fraction.

$0.32 = \dfrac{32}{100}$. This cancels down to $\dfrac{8}{25}$.

Example 2   Express $\frac{3}{8}$ as a decimal. $\frac{3}{8} = 3 \div 8 = 0.375$

$$
\begin{array}{r}
0.375 \\
8\,\overline{\smash)3.^30^60^40}
\end{array}
$$ Notice how the extra zeros have been added.

1   Change each of these decimals to fractions, cancelling down where possible.
   a   0.3   **b**   0.8   **c**   0.9   **d**   0.07   **e**   0.08
   f   0.15   **g**   0.75   **h**   0.48   **i**   0.32   **j**   0.27

2   Change each of these fractions to decimals.
   a $\frac{1}{4}$ **b** $\frac{2}{5}$ **c** $\frac{7}{10}$ **d** $\frac{9}{20}$ **e** $\frac{7}{8}$

3   Put each of the following sets of numbers in order with the smallest first. It is easier to change the fractions into decimals first.
   a $0.3, 0.2, \frac{2}{5}$ **b** $\frac{7}{10}, 0.8, 0.6$ **c** $0.4, \frac{1}{4}, 0.2$
   d $\frac{3}{10}, 0.32, 0.29$ **e** $0.81, \frac{4}{5}, 0.78$

HOMEWORK 9A

Example 1   Simplify 5 : 2 0.

$5 : 20 = 1 : 4$ (Divide both side of the ratio by 5).

Example 2   Simplify 20p : £2.

(Change to a common unit) 20p : 200p = 1:10

Example 3   A garden is divided into lawn and shrubs in the ratio 3 : 2.

The lawn covers $\frac{3}{5}$ of the garden and the shrubs cover $\frac{2}{5}$ of the garden.

1   Express each of the following ratios in their simplest form.
a 3 : 9	**b** 5 : 25	**c** 4 : 24	**d** 10 : 30	**e** 6 : 9
f 12 : 20	**g** 25 : 40	**h** 30 : 4	**i** 14 : 35	**j** 125 : 50

2   Express each of the following ratios of quantities in their simplest form. (Remember to change to a common unit where necessary.)
a £2 to £8	**b** £12 to £16	**c** 25 g to 200 g
d 6 miles : 15 miles	**e** 20 cm : 50 cm	**f** 80p : £1.50
g 1 kg : 300g	**h** 40 seconds : 2 minutes	**i** 9 hours : 1 day
j 4 mm : 2cm		

3   £20 is shared out between Bob and Kathryn in the ratio 1 : 3.
   a   What fraction of the £20 does Bob receive?
   b   What fraction of the £20 does Kathryn receive?

4   In a class of students, the ratio of boys to girls is 2 : 3.
   a   What fraction of the class is boys?
   b   What fraction of the class is girls?

5   Pewter is an alloy containing lead and tin in the ratio 1 : 9.
   a   What fraction of pewter is lead?
   b   What fraction of pewter is tin?

 HOMEWORK 9B

Example   Divide £40 between Peter and Hitan in the ratio 2 : 3

Changing the ratio to fractions gives
Peter's share = $\frac{2}{5}$ and Hitan's share = $\frac{3}{5}$
So, Peter receives $\frac{2}{5} \times £40 = £16$ and Hitan receives $\frac{3}{5} \times £40 = £24$

1   Divide each of the following amounts in the given ratios.
a £10 in the ratio 1 : 4	**b** £12 in the ratio 1 : 2
c £40 in the ratio 1 : 3	**d** 60 g in the ratio 1 : 5
e 10 hours in the ratio 1 : 9	**f** 25 kg in the ratio 2 : 3
g 30 days the ratio 3 : 2	**h** 70 m in the ratio 3 : 4
i £5 in the ratio 3 : 7	**j** 1 day in the ratio 5 : 3

2 The ratio of female to male members of a Sports Centre is 3 : 1. The total number of members of the Centre is 400.

    a How many members are female?   **b** How many members are male?

3 A 20 metre length of cloth is cut into two pieces in the ratio 1 : 9. How long is each piece?

4 James collects beer mats and the ratio of British mats to foreign mats is 5 : 2. He has 1400 beer mats in his collection. How many foreign beer mats does he have?

5 Patrick and Jane share out a box of sweets in the ratio of their ages. Patrick is 9 years old and Jane is 11 years old. If there are 100 sweets in the box, how many does Patrick get?

★6 For her birthday Reena is given £30. She decides to spend four times as much as she saves. How much does she save?

7 Mrs Megson calculates that her quarterly electric and gas bills are in the ratio 5 : 6. The total she pays for both bills is £66. How much is each bill?

8 You can simplify a ratio by changing it into the form 1 : n. For example, 5 : 7 can be rewritten as 5 : 7 = 1 : 1.4 by dividing each side of the ratio by 5. Rewrite each of the following ratios in the form 1 : n.

    a 2 : 3   **b** 2 : 5   **c** 4 : 5   **d** 5 : 8   **e** 10 : 21

HOMEWORK 9C

Example Two business partners, John and Ben, divided their total profit in the ratio 3 : 5. John received £2100. How much did Ben get?

    John's £2100 was $\frac{3}{8}$ of the total profit.

    So, $\frac{1}{8}$ of the total profit = £2100 ÷ 3 = £700.

    Therefore, Ben's share, which was $\frac{5}{8}$, amounted to £700 × 5 = £3500.

1 Peter and Margaret's ages are in the ratio 4 : 5. If Peter is 16 years old, how old is Margaret?

2 Cans of lemonade and packets of crisps were bought for the school disco in the ratio 3 : 2. The organiser bought 120 cans of lemonade. How many packets of crisps did she buy?

3 In his restaurant, Manuel is making 'Sangria', a drink made from red wine and iced soda water, mixed in the ratio 2 : 3. Manuel uses 10 litres of red wine.

    a How many litres of soda water does he use?

    b How many litres of Sangria does he make?

4 Cupro-nickel coins are minted by mixing copper and nickel in the ratio 4 : 1.

    a How much copper is needed to mix with 20 kg of nickel?

    b How much nickel is needed to mix with 20 kg of copper?

5 The ratio of male to female spectators at a school inter-form football match is 2 : 1. If 60 boys watched the game, how many spectators were there in total?

★6 Marmalade is made from sugar and oranges in the ratio 3 : 5. A jar of 'Savilles' marmalade contains 120 g of sugar.

    a How many grams of oranges are in the jar?

    b How many grams of marmalade are in the jar?

★7 Each year Abbey School holds a sponsored walk for charity. The money raised is shared between a local charity and a national charity in the ratio 1 : 2. Last year the school gave £2000 to the local charity.
  a How much did the school give to the national charity?
  b How much did the school raise in total?

HOMEWORK 9D

The relationship between speed, time and distance can be expressed in three ways:

$$\text{Distance} = \text{Speed} \times \text{Time} \qquad \text{Speed} = \frac{\text{Distance}}{\text{Time}} \qquad \text{Time} = \frac{\text{Distance}}{\text{Speed}}$$

Example Sean is going to drive from Newcastle upon Tyne to Nottingham, a distance of 190 miles. He estimates that he will drive at an average speed of 50 mph. How long will it take him?

Sean's time $= \frac{190}{50} = 3.8$ hours

Change the 0.8 hours to minutes by multiplying by 60, to give 48 minutes. So, the time for Sean's journey will be 3 hours 48 minutes.

Remember When you calculate a time and get a decimal answer, do not mistake the decimal part for minutes. You must either

- leave the time as a decimal number and give the unit as hours, or
- change the decimal part to minutes by multiplying it by 60 (1 hour = 60 minutes) and give the answer in hours and minutes.

1 A cyclist travels a distance of 60 miles in 4 hours. What was her average speed?

2 How far along a motorway will you travel if you drive at an average speed of 60 mph for 3 hours?

3 Mr Baylis drives on a business trip from Manchester to London in $4\frac{1}{2}$ hours. The distance he travels is 207 miles. What is his average speed?

4 The distance from Leeds to Birmingham is 125 miles. The train I catch travels at an average speed of 50 mph. If I catch the 11.30am train in Leeds, at what time would I expect to be in Birmingham?

5 Copy and complete the following table.

	Distance travelled	Time taken	Average speed
a	240 miles	8 hours	
b	150 km	3 hours	
c		4 hours	5 mph
d		$2\frac{1}{2}$ hours	20 km/h
e	1300 miles		400 mph
f	90 km		25 km/h

★6 A coach travels at an average speed of 60 km/h for 2 hours on a motorway and then slows down in a town centre to do the last 30 minutes of a journey at an average speed of 20 km/h.
  a What is the total distance of this journey?
  b What is the average speed of the coach over the whole journey?

★7 Hilary cycles to work each day. She cycles the first 5 miles at an average speed of 15 mph and then cycles the last mile in 10 minutes.
  a How long does it take her to get to work?
  b What is her average speed for the whole journey?

★8 Martha drives home from work in 1 hour 15 minutes. She drives home at an average speed of 36 mph.
  a Change 1 hour 15 minutes to decimal time in hours.
  b How far is it from Martha's work to her home?

HOMEWORK 9E

Example   If eight pens cost £2.64, what is the cost of five pens?

First find the cost of one pen. This is £2.64 ÷ 8 = £0.33
The cost of five pens is £0.33 × 5 = £1.65

1 If four video tapes cost £3.20, what would ten video tapes cost?

2 Five oranges cost 90p. Find the cost of twelve oranges.

3 Dylan earns £18.60 in 3 hours. How much will he earn in 8 hours?

4 Barbara bought 12 postcards for 900 pesetas when she was on holiday in Tenerife.
  a How many pesetas would she have paid if she had only bought 9 postcards?
  b How many postcards could she have bought with a 2000 pesetas note?

5 Five 'Day-Rover' bus tickets cost £8.50.
  a What is the cost of 16 tickets?
  b How many tickets can be bought for £20?

6 A car uses 8 litres of petrol on a trip of 72 miles.
  a How much would be used on a trip of 54 miles?
  b How far would the car go on a full tank of 45 litres?

7 It takes a photocopier 18 seconds to produce 12 copies. How long will it take to produce 32 copies?

★8 Val has a recipe for making 12 flapjacks.
     100 g margarine
     4 tablespoons golden syrup
     80 g granulated sugar
     200 g rolled oats
  a What is the recipe for
     i 6 flapjacks   **ii** 24 flapjacks   **iii** 30 flapjacks
  b What is the maximum number of flapjacks she can make if she has 1 kg of each ingredient?

Example   There are two different-sized packets of Whito soap powder at a supermarket. The medium size contains 800 g and costs £1.60 and the large size contains 2.5 kg and costs £4.75. Which is the better buy?

Find the weight per unit cost for both packets.
Medium: $800 \div 160 = 5$ g per pence
Large: $2500 \div 475 = 5.26$ g per pence

From these we see that there is more weight per pence with the large size, which means that the large size is the better buy.

1   Compare the following pairs of product and state which is the better buy and why.
a   Tomato ketchup: a medium bottle which is 200 g for 55p or a large bottle which is 350 g for 87p.
b   Milk chocolate: a 125 g bar at 77p or a 200 g bar at 92p.
c   Coffee: a 750 g tin at £11.95 or a 500 g tin at £7.85.
d   Honey: a large jar which is 900 g for £2.35 or a small jar which is 225 g for 65p.

2   Boxes of 'Wetherels' teabags are sold in three different sizes.

Small

80 teabags
£1.44

Medium
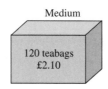
120 teabags
£2.10

Large
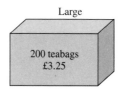
200 teabags
£3.25

Which size of teabags gives the best value for money?

3   Bottles of 'Cola' are sold in different sizes. Copy and complete the table.

Size of bottle	Price	Cost per litre
$\frac{1}{2}$ litre	36p	
$1\frac{1}{2}$ litres	99p	
2 litres	£1.40	
3 litres	£1.95	

Which bottle gives the best value for money?

★4   The following 'special offers' were being promoted by a supermarket.

Only £1.99 each

Cornflakes
750 g
£1.99

Buy 3 for the price of 2

Cornflakes
500 g
£1.69

Which offer is the better value for money? Explain why.

HOMEWORK 10A

1 Copy these shapes and draw on the lines of symmetry for each one. If it will help you, use tracing paper or a mirror to check your answers.

a   **b**    **c**

d   **e**

2 Copy this regular hexagon and draw on all the lines of symmetry.

3 Copy these flow chart symbols and draw on all the lines of symmetry for each one.

a    **b**   **c**

d   **e**

4 Write down the number of lines of symmetry for each of these flags.

a    **b**    **c**

5 How many lines of symmetry do each of these letters have?

a A   **b** E   **c** H   **d** T   **e** Y

★6 Draw three copies of the diagram below
    a Shade in two more squares so that the diagram has no lines of symmetry.
    b Shade in two more squares so that the diagram has exactly one line of symmetry.
    c Shade in two more squares so that the diagram has exactly two lines of symmetry.

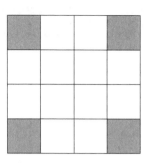

 HOMEWORK 10B

1 Copy these shapes and write below each one the order of rotational symmetry. If it will help you, use tracing paper.

a   **b**   **c**

d   **e**

2 Write down the order of rotational symmetry for each of these shapes.

a   **b**   **c**

d   **e**

3 Write down the order of rotational symmetry for each of the symbols.

a   **b**   **c**   **d**   **e**

4 The capital letter A fits exactly onto itself only once. So, its order of rotational symmetry is 1. This means that it has no rotational symmetry. Copy these capital letters of the alphabet and write the order of rotational symmetry below each one.

a E   **b** H   **c** I   **d** L   **e** N

f Q   **g** S   **h** Z

★5 Draw two copies of the diagram
    a Shade in two more squares so that the diagram has rotational symmetry of order 2 and no lines of symmetry.
    b Shade in two more squares so that the diagram has rotational symmetry of order 1 and exactly 1 line of symmetry.

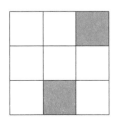

1 Find the number of planes of symmetry in each of these 3-D shapes.

a

b

c

d

2 This 3-D shape has two planes of symmetry. Draw diagrams to show where they are.

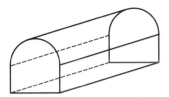

3 The diagram shows half of a 3-D shape. Draw the complete shape so that the shaded part forms a plane of symmetry. What name do we give to this 3-D shape?

4 How many planes of symmetry does each of the following have?

a

b

c

d

Chapter 11   Averages

The mode is the value that occurs the most in a set of data. That is, it is the value with the highest frequency.

Example   Terry scored the following number of goals in 12 school football matches:

1   2   1   0   1   0   0   1   2   1   0   2

The number which occurs most often in this list is 1. So, the mode is 1.

We can also say that the modal score is 1.

1 Find the mode for each set of data.

 a 3, 1, 2, 5, 6, 4, 1, 5, 1, 3, 6, 1, 4, 2, 3, 2, 4, 2, 4, 2, 6, 5

 b 17, 11, 12, 15, 11, 13, 18, 14, 17, 15, 13, 15, 16, 14

 c 110, 10, 101, 10, 111, 110, 11, 101, 11, 111, 11, 101, 101, 111

 d 1, –3, 3, 2, –1, 1, –3, –2, 3, –1, 2, 1, –1, 1, 2

 e 7, $6\frac{1}{2}$, 6, $7\frac{1}{2}$, 8, $5\frac{1}{2}$, $6\frac{1}{2}$, 6, 7, $6\frac{1}{2}$, 7, $6\frac{1}{2}$, 6, $7\frac{1}{2}$

2 Find the modal category for each set of data.

 a I, A, E, U, A, O, A, E, U, A, I, A, E, I, E, O, E, I, E, O

 b ITV, C4, BBC1, C5, BBC2, C4, BBC1, C5, ITV, C4, BBC1, C4, ITV

 c ↑, →, ↑, ←, ↓, →, ←, ↑, ←, →, ↓, ←, ←, ↑, →, ↓

 d ♥, ♣, ♦, ♣, ♠, ♥, ♣, ♦, ♣, ♦, ♥, ♠

 e ¥, €, £, €, $, £, ¥, €, £, $, €, £, $, €

3 Farmer Giles kept a record of the number of eggs his hens laid. His data is shown on the diagram below.

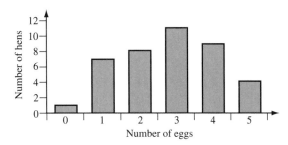

 a How many hens did Farmer Giles have?

 b What is the mode of the number of eggs laid?

 c How many eggs were laid altogether?

★**4** The grouped frequency table shows the number of marks a class of students obtained in a Spelling Test out of 30 marks.

Number of marks	Frequency
1–5	1
6–10	2
11–15	4
16–20	8
21–25	10
26–30	5

 a How many pupils are in the class?

 b Write down the modal class for the number of marks.

 c Stan looked at the table and said that at least one person got full marks. Explain why he may be wrong.

★5 The data shows the times, to the nearest minute, of how long 30 shoppers had to wait in the queue at a check-out of a supermarket.

1   3   8   12   7   4   0   9   10   15   8   1   2   7   4
2   4   7   1   0   5   4   8   4   10   7   5   4   1   5

a Copy and complete the grouped frequency table.

Time in minutes	Tally	Frequency
0–3		
4–7		
8–11		
12–15		

b Draw a bar chart to illustrate the data.

c How many shoppers had to wait more than seven minutes?

d Write down the modal class for the time that the shoppers had to wait?

e How could the supermarket manager decrease the waiting time of the shoppers?

HOMEWORK 11B

The median is the value at the middle of a list of values after they have been put in order of size, from lowest to highest.

Example 1 Find the median for the following list of numbers:

2, 3, 5, 6, 1, 2, 3, 4, 5, 4, 6
Putting the list in numerical order gives
1, 2, 2, 3, 3, 4, 4, 5, 5, 6, 6
There are 11 numbers in the list, so the middle of the list is the 6th number.
Therefore, the median is 4.

Example 2 The ages of 20 people attending a conference were as follows:

28, 32, 46, 23, 28, 34, 52, 61, 45, 34, 39, 50, 26, 44, 60, 53, 31, 25, 37, 48
Draw a stem-and-leaf diagram and hence find the median age of the group.
Taking the tens to be the 'stem' and the units to be the 'leaves', the stem-and-leaf diagram is shown below. (**2 | 3** means 23)

```
2 | 3 5 6 8 8
3 | 1 2 4 4 7 9
4 | 4 5 6 8
5 | 0 2 3
6 | 0 1
```

There is an even number of values in this list, so the middle of the list is between the two central values, 37 and 39. Therefore, the median is the value which is exactly midway between 37 and 39. Hence, the median is 38.

1 Find the median for each set of data.

a 18, 12, 15, 19, 13, 16, 10, 14, 17, 20, 11

b 22, 28, 42, 37, 26, 51, 30, 34, 43

c 1, –3, 0, 2, –4, 3, –1, 2, 0, 1, –2

d 12, 4, 16, 12, 14, 8, 10, 4, 6, 14

e 1.7, 2.1, 1.1, 2.7, 1.3, 0.9, 1.5, 1.8, 2.3, 1.4

2 The weights of eleven men in a local rugby team were as follows:

81 kg, 85 kg, 82 kg, 71 kg, 62 kg, 63 kg, 62 kg, 64 kg, 70 kg, 87 kg, 74 kg

   a Find the median of their weights.
   b Find the mode of their weights.
   c Which is the better average to use? Explain your answer.

3 The bar chart shows the scores obtained in 20 throws of a dice.

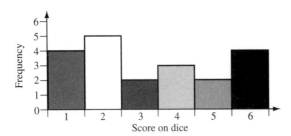

   a Write down the modal score.
   b Find the median score. Remember you must take into account all the scores.
   c Do you think that the dice is biased? Explain your answer.

4 **a** Write down a list of seven numbers which has a median of 10 and a mode of 20.
   b Write down a list of eight numbers which has a median of 10 and a mode of 20

★**5** The marks of 21 students in a Science modular test were as follows:

45, 62, 27, 77, 40, 55, 80, 87, 49, 57, 35, 52, 59, 78, 48, 67, 43, 68, 38, 72, 81

Draw a stem-and-leaf diagram to find the median.

★**6** Jack is doing his Statistics Coursework based on 'Pulse Rates'. One of his hypotheses is that a person's pulse rate increases after exercise. To test his hypothesis he asks 31 students in a PE lesson to take their pulse rate at the start of the lesson and again at the end of the lesson. He records the data on an observation sheet and then illustrates it on a back to back stem-and-leaf diagram.

Before exercise		*After exercise*
9, 9, 8, 5, 3	**5**	
8, 8, 5, 4, 3, 2, 1	**6**	
9, 8, 7, 7, 4, 2, 2, 2, 0	**7**	1, 1, 2
9, 6, 5, 2, 2	**8**	0, 0, 2, 7, 8
8, 7, 5	**9**	0, 2, 2, 3, 5, 5, 8
4, 2	**10**	1, 2, 4, 5, 8, 9
	11	4, 6, 8, 9
	12	2, 5, 6
	13	8, 9
	14	4

(| **7** | 2 means 72 beats per minute)

   a Find the median pulse rate of the students at the start of the lesson.
   b Find the median pulse rate of the students at the end of the lesson.
   c What conclusions can Jack draw from the stem-and-leaf diagram?

The mean of a set of data is the sum of all the values in the set divided by the total number of values in the set.

That is: mean $= \dfrac{\text{Sum of all values}}{\text{Total number of values}}$

Example   Find the mean of 4, 8, 7, 5, 9, 4, 8, 3

Sum of all the values $= 4 + 8 + 7 + 5 + 9 + 4 + 8 + 3 = 48$
Total number of values $= 8$
Therefore, mean $= 48 \div 8 = 6$

1   Find the mean for each set of data.
   a   4, 2, 5, 8, 6, 4, 2, 3, 5, 1
   b   21, 25, 27, 20, 23, 26, 28, 22
   c   324, 423, 342, 234, 432, 243
   d   2.5, 3.6, 3.1, 4.2, 3.5, 2.9
   e   1, 4, 3, 0, 1, 2, 5, 0, 2, 4, 2, 0

2   Calculate the mean for each set of data, giving your answer correct to one decimal place.
   a   17, 24, 18, 32, 16, 28, 20
   b   92, 101, 98, 102, 95, 104, 99, 96, 103
   c   9.8, 9.3, 10.1, 8.7, 11.8, 10.5, 8.5
   d   202, 212, 220, 102, 112, 201, 222
   e   4, 2, –1, 0, 1, –3, 5, 0, –1, 4, –2, 1

3   A group of eight people took part in a marathon to raise money for charity. Their times to run the marathon were:
   2 hours 40 minutes, 3 hours 6 minutes, 2 hours 50 minutes, 3 hours 25 minutes,
   4 hours 32 minutes, 3 hours 47 minutes, 2 hours 46 minutes, 3 hours 18 minutes
Calculate their mean time in hours and minutes.

4   The monthly wages of 11 full-time staff who work in a restaurant are as follows: £820,
   £520, £860, £2000, £800, £1600, £760, £810, £620, £570, £650
   a   Find their median wage.
   b   Calculate their mean wage.
   c   How many of the staff earn more than
      i the median wage   **ii** the mean wage?
   d   Which is the better average to use? Give a reason for your answer.

★5   The table shows the percentage marks which ten students obtained in Paper 1 and Paper 2 of their GCSE Mathematics examination.

	Ann	Bridget	Carole	Daniel	Edwin	Fay	George	Hannah	Imman	Joseph
Paper 1	72	61	43	92	56	62	73	56	38	67
Paper 2	81	57	49	85	62	61	70	66	48	51

   a   Calculate the mean mark for Paper 1.
   b   Calculate the mean mark for Paper 2.
   c   Which student obtained marks closest to the mean on both papers?
   d   How many students were above the mean mark on both papers?

★**6** The number of runs that a cricketer scored in seven innings were:
48, 32, 0, 62, 11, 21, 43
- **a** Calculate the mean number of runs in the seven innings.
- **b** After eight innings his mean score increased to 33 runs per innings. How many runs did he score in his eighth innings?

The range for a set of data is the highest value in the set minus the lowest value in the set.

Example Rachel's marks in ten mental arithmetic tests were 4, 4, 7, 6, 6, 5, 7, 6, 9, 6
Her mean mark is $60 \div 10 = 6$ marks, and her range is $9 - 4 = 5$ marks.
Robert's marks in the same tests were 6, 7, 6, 8, 5, 6, 5, 6, 5, 6
His mean mark is $60 \div 10 = 6$ marks, and his range is $8 - 5 = 3$ marks.
Although the means are the same, Robert has a smaller range. This shows that Robert's results are more consistent.

1 Find the range for each set of data.
- **a** 23, 18, 27, 14, 25, 19, 20, 26, 17, 24
- **b** 92, 89, 101, 96, 100, 96, 102, 88, 99, 95
- **c** 14, 30, 44, 25, 36, 27, 15, 42, 27, 12, 40, 31, 34, 24
- **d** 3.2, 4.8, 5.7, 3.1, 3.8, 4.9, 5.8, 3.5, 5.6, 3.7
- **e** 5, −4, 0, 2, −5, −1, 4, −3, 2, 2, 0, 1, −4, 0, −2

2 The table shows the ages of a group of students on an 'Outward Bound' course at a Youth Hostel.

Age	14	15	16	17	18	19
Number of students	2	3	8	5	6	1

- **a** How many students were on the course?
- **b** Write down the modal age of the students.
- **c** What is the range of their ages?
- **d** Draw a bar chart to illustrate the data.

3 A travel brochure shows the average monthly temperatures, in °C, for the island of Crete.

Month	April	May	June	July	August	September	October
Temperature °C	68	74	78	83	82	75	72

- **a** Calculate the mean of these temperatures.
- **b** Write down the range of these temperatures.
- **c** The mean temperature for the island of Corfu was 77 °C and the range was 20 °C. Compare the temperatures for the two islands.

4 The table shows the daily attendance of three forms of 30 students over a week.

	Monday	**Tuesday**	**Wednesday**	**Thursday**	**Friday**
Form 10KG	25	25	26	27	27
Form 10RH	22	23	30	26	24
Form 10PB	24	29	28	25	29

- **a** Calculate the mean attendance for each form.
- **b** Write down the range for the attendance of each form.
- **c** Which form had **i** the best attendance **ii** the most consistent attendance? Give reasons for your answers.

★5 The back to back stem-and-leaf diagram shows the marks of 30 pupils in one of their Key Stage 3 English tests.

Boys		Girls
	1	8
8, 7, 6, 4	**2**	4, 5, 7, 9
9, 7, 7, 4, 1, 0	**3**	1, 4, 7, 8
6, 5, 2, 0	**4**	0, 1, 3, 4, 7
2	**5**	4

(| **4** | 2 means 42 marks)

a Find the median mark for the boys and for the girls.

b Write down the range of the marks for the boys and for the girls.

c Compare the results of the boys and the girls.

HOMEWORK 11E

1 **a** For each set of data find the mode, the median and the mean.

   i   6, 4, 5, 6, 2, 3, 2, 4, 5, 6, 1

   ii   14, 15, 15, 16, 15, 15, 14, 16, 15, 16, 15

   iii   31, 34, 33, 32, 46, 29, 30, 32, 31, 32, 33

   b For each set of data decide which average is the best one to use and give a reason.

2 A supermarket sells oranges in bags of ten.

   The weights of each orange in a selected bag were as follows:

   134 g, 135 g, 142 g, 153 g, 156 g, 132 g, 135 g, 140 g, 148 g, 155 g

   a Find the mode, the median and the mean for the weight of the oranges.

   b The supermarket wanted to state the average weight on each bag they sold. Which of the three averages would you advise the supermarket to use? Explain why.

★**3** The weights, in kilograms, of players in a school football team are as follows:

   68, 72, 74, 68, 71, 78, 53, 67, 72, 77, 70

   a Find the median weight of the team.

   b Find the mean weight of the team.

   c Which average is the better one to use? Explain why.

★**4** Jez is a member of a pub quiz team and, in the last eight games, his total points were:

   62, 58, 24, 47, 64, 52, 60, 65

   a Find the median for the number of points he scored over the eight weeks.

   b Find the mean for the number of points he scored over the eight weeks.

   c The team captain wanted to know the average for each member of the team. Which average would Jez use? Give a reason for your answer.

HOMEWORK 11F

Example A survey was done on the number of people in each car leaving the Meadowhall Shopping Centre, in Sheffield. The results are summarised in the table below.

Number of people in each car	1	2	3	4	5	6
Frequency	45	98	121	76	52	13

Find the mean of the number of people in a car.

The mean number of people in a car is found by adding together all the people and then dividing this total by the number of cars surveyed. This is best done by completing the following table.

Number in a car (x)	Frequency (f)	$x \times f$
1	45	45
2	198	396
3	121	363
4	76	304
5	52	260
6	13	78
Totals	**505**	**1446**

Hence, the mean number of people in a car is $1446 \div 505 = 2.9$ (1 dp).

1 The frequency table shows the number of children in 30 families.

Number of children	0	1	2	3	4
Frequency	4	12	9	3	2

Calculate the mean number of children per family. Give your answer to 1 decimal place.

2 The frequency table shows the score on a dice when it is thrown 60 times.

Score	1	2	3	4	5	6
Frequency	12	9	10	8	11	10

a Write down the range of the scores.
b Write down the modal score.
c Calculate the mean score.

3 The frequency table shows the number of goals Albion Rovers scored in the first 20 matches of the season.

Number of goals	0	1	2	3	4
Frequency	3	5	8	3	1

a Write down the mode for the number of goals scored.
b Find the median for the number of goals scored.
c Calculate the mean for the number of goals scored.

★4 The bar chart shows the number of words on each line in one of Shakespeare's sonnets.

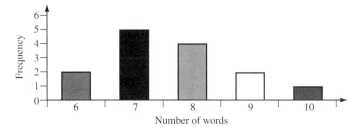

a How many lines are there in a sonnet?
b Calculate the mean number of words per line in the sonnet. Give your answer to 1 decimal place.

Chapter 12 — Percentage

HOMEWORK 12A

Example 1   As a fraction $32\% = \frac{32}{100}$ which can be cancelled down to $\frac{8}{25}$

Example 2   As a decimal $65\% = 65 \div 100 = 0.65$

1   Write each percentage as a fraction in its lowest terms.

a 10%	**b** 40%	**c** 25%	**d** 15%	**e** 75%	**f** 35%
g 12%	**h** 28%	**i** 56%	**j** 18%	**k** 42%	**l** 6%

2   Write each percentage as a decimal.

a 87%	**b** 25%	**c** 33%	**d** 5%	**e** 1%	**f** 72%
g 58%	**h** 17.5%	**i** 8.5%	**j** 68.2%	**k** 150%	**l** 132%

3   Copy and complete the table.

Percentage	Fraction	Decimal
10%		
20%		
30%		
		0.4
		0.5
		0.6
	$\frac{7}{10}$	
	$\frac{8}{10}$	
	$\frac{9}{10}$	

4   If 45% of pupils walk to school, what percentage do not walk to school?

5   If 84% of the families in a village own at least one car, what percentage of the families do not own a car?

6   In a local election, of all the people who voted, 48% voted for Mrs Slater, 29% voted for Mr Rhodes and the remainder voted for Mr Mulley. What percentage voted for Mr Mulley?

7   From his gross salary, Mr Hardy pays 20% Income Tax, 6% Superannuation and 5% National Insurance. What percentage is his net pay?

8   Approximately what percentage of each can is filled with oil?

a    **b**    **c**

Example   Calculate 12% of 54 kg.

Method 1. $12 \div 100 \times 54 = 6.48$ kg
Method 2.   Using the calculator % key.

1 ⎢ 2 ⎢ % ⎢ × ⎢ 5 ⎢ 4 ⎢ =

1 Calculate the following.

a	25% of £200	**b**	10% of £120	**c**	53% of 400 kg	**d**	75% of 84 cm
e	22% of £84	**f**	71% of 250 g	**g**	24% of £3	**h**	95% of 320 m
i	6% of £42	**j**	17.5% of £56	**k**	8.5% of 160 l	**l**	37.2% of £800

2 During one week at a Test Centre, 320 people took their driving test and 65% passed. How many people passed?

3 A school has 250 pupils on roll in each year and the attendance record on one day for each year group was as follows:
Year 7   96%,   Year 8   92%,   Year 9   84%,   Year 10   88%,   Year 11   80%
How many pupils were present in each year group on that day?

4 A certain type of stainless steel consists of 84% iron, 14% chromium and 2% carbon (by weight). How much of each is in 450 tonnes of stainless steel?

★5 Value Added Tax (VAT) is added on to most goods purchased at the rate of $17\frac{1}{2}$%. How much VAT will be added on to the following bills:

a a restaurant bill for £40   **b** a telephone bill for £82

c a car repair bill for £240?

★6 An insurance firm sells house insurance and the annual premiums are usually at a cost of 0.5% of the value of the house. What will be the annual premium for a house valued at £120 000?

HOMEWORK 12C

Example   Increase £6 by 5%.

Method 1.   Find 5% of £6: $(5 \div 100) \times 6 = £0.30$
             Add the £0.30 to the original amount: $£6 + £0.30 = £6.30$

Method 2.   Using the calculator % key.

⎢ 6 ⎢ + ⎢ 5 ⎢ % ⎢ =

1 Increase each of the following by the given percentage. (Use any method you like.)

a	£80 by 5%	**b**	£150 by 10%	**c**	800 m by 15%	**d**	320 kg by 25%
e	£42 by 30%	**f**	£24 by 65%	**g**	120 cm by 18%	**h**	£32 by 46%
i	550g by 85%	**j**	£72 by 72%					

2 Mr Kent, who was on a salary of £32 500, was given a pay rise of 4%. What is his new salary?

3 Copy and complete this electricity bill.

	Total charges
Fixed charges	£13.00
840 units @ 6.45 p per unit	
1720 units @ 2.45 p per unit	
Total charges	
VAT @ 5%	
Total to pay	

4 A bank pays 8% simple interest on the money that each saver keeps in a savings account for a year. Miss Pettica puts £2000 in this account for three years. How much will she have in her account after

    a 1 year   **b** 2 years   **c** 3 years?

★5 VAT is a tax that the Government adds to the price of goods sold. At the moment it is 17.5% on all goods. Calculate the price of the following gifts Mrs Dow purchased from a gift catalogue, after VAT of 17.5% has been added.

Gift	Pre-VAT price
Travel alarm clock	£18.00
Ladies' purse wallet	£15.20
Pet's luxury towel	£12.80
Silver-plated bookmark	£6.40

 HOMEWORK 12D

Example Decrease £6 by 5%.

    Method 1. Find 5% of £6: $(5 \div 100) \times 6 = £0.30$
                     Subtract the £0.30 from the original amount: $£6 - £0.30 = £5.70$

    Method 2. Using the calculator % key.

1 Decrease each of the following by the given percentage. (Use any method you like.)

    a £20 by 10%   **b** £150 by 20%   **c** 90 kg by 30%   **d** 500 m by 12%
    e £260 by 5%   **f** 80 cm by 25%   **g** 400 g by 42%   **h** £425 by 23%
    i 48 kg by 75%   **j** £63 by 37%

2 Mrs Denghali buys a new car from a garage for £8400. The garage owner tells her that the value of the car will lose 24% after one year. What will be the value of the car after one year?

★3 The population of a village in 1995 was 2400. In 2000 the population had decreased by 12%. What was the population of the village in 2000?

★4 A Travel Agent is offering a 15% discount on holidays. How much will the advertised holiday now cost?

NEW YORK FOR A WEEK
£540

★5

| New Year's Sale: |
| All prices reduced by 20% |

Find the sale price of the following goods in the sale.

a a shirt at £30   **b** a suit at £130   **c** a pair of shoes at £42

HOMEWORK 12E

Example 1   Express $\frac{4}{5}$ as a percentage.

$$4 \div 5 \times 100\% = 80\%$$

Example 2   Express 0.68 as a percentage.

$$0.68 \times 100\% = 68\%$$

1 Change each of these fractions into a percentage.

   a $\frac{1}{5}$ **b** $\frac{3}{4}$ **c** $\frac{7}{10}$ **d** $\frac{1}{4}$ **e** $\frac{3}{10}$

   f $\frac{17}{100}$ **g** $\frac{9}{20}$ **h** $\frac{13}{20}$ **i** $\frac{23}{50}$ **j** $\frac{11}{25}$

2 Change each of these fractions into a percentage. Give your answers to one decimal place.

   a $\frac{1}{3}$ **b** $\frac{2}{3}$ **c** $\frac{1}{6}$ **d** $\frac{5}{6}$ **e** $\frac{5}{12}$

3 Change each of these decimals into a percentage.

   a 0.9   **b** 0.3   **c** 0.58   **d** 0.79   **e** 0.98

   f 0.24   **g** 0.08   **h** 0.01   **i** 0.125   **j** 1.3

4 Martin scored 48 points out of a possible 60 points in a swimming competition.

   a Write his score as a fraction.   **b** Write his score as a decimal.

   c Write his score as a percentage.

5 Put these numbers in order of size, with the smallest first.

   a $\frac{1}{4}$, 0.3, 20%   **b** $\frac{1}{10}$, 3%, 0.05   **c** 0.85, 80%, $\frac{3}{4}$

★**6** The land surface of the Earth is approximately $\frac{7}{10}$.

   a What percentage of the Earth's surface is land?

   b What percentage of the Earth's surface is water?

7 Convert each of the following test scores into a percentage. Give each answer to the nearest whole number.

Subject	Result	Percentage
Mathematics	65 out of 80	
Science	37 out of 60	
English	41 out of 75	
French	23 out of 30	
German	66 out of 120	

Example   Express £6 as a percentage of £40.

Method 1.   Set up the fraction $\frac{6}{40}$ and multiply it by 100. $6 \div 40 \times 100\% = 15\%$

Method 2.   Using the calculator % key.

1   Express each of the following as a percentage. Give your answers to 1 decimal place where necessary.

   a   £8 of £40   **b**   20 kg of 80 kg   **c**   5 m of 50 m

   d   £15 of £20   **e**   400 g of 500 g   **f**   23 cm of 50 cm

   g   £12 of £36   **h**   18 minutes of 1 hour   **i**   £27 of £40

   j   5 days of 3 weeks

2   What percentage of these shapes is shaded?

   a   **b**

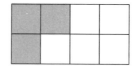

3   In a class of 30 pupils, 18 are girls.

   a   What percentage of the class are girls?

   b   What percentage of the class are boys?

4   The area of a farm is 820 hectares. The farmer uses 240 hectares for pasture.
   What percentage of the farm land is used for pasture? Give your answer to 1 decimal place.

5   Find, to one decimal place, the percentage profit on each of the following.

	Item	Retail price (Selling price)	Wholesale price (Price the shop paid)
a	Micro Hi-Fi System	£250	£150
b	CD Radio Cassette	£90	£60
c	MiniDisc Player	£44.99	£30
d	Cordless Headphones	£29.99	£18

Chapter 13   More algebra

Example   Solve $3x - 4 = 11$ using an inverse flow diagram:

The flow diagram for the equation is:

Inverse flow diagram:

$$x \longleftarrow \boxed{\div 3} \longleftarrow \boxed{+4} \longleftarrow 11$$

Put through the value on the right-hand side:

$$5 \longleftarrow \boxed{\div 3} \longleftarrow \boxed{+4} \longleftarrow 11$$

The answer is $x = 5$

Checking the answer gives $3 \times 5 - 4 = 11$ which is correct.

Solve each of the following equations using inverse flow diagrams. Do not forget to check that each answer works in the original equation.

1 $2x + 5 = 13$ **2** $3x - 2 = 4$ **3** $2x - 7 = 3$ **4** $3y - 9 = 9$

5 $5a + 1 = 11$ **6** $4x + 5 = 21$ **7** $6y + 6 = 24$ **8** $5x + 4 = 9$

9 $8x - 10 = 30$ **10** $\dfrac{x}{2} + 1 = 4$ **11** $\dfrac{a}{2} - 2 = 3$ **12** $\dfrac{c}{3} + 2 = 8$

13 $\dfrac{x}{3} - 3 = 1$ **14** $\dfrac{m}{3} - 1 = 2$ **15** $\dfrac{z}{5} + 6 = 10$

HOMEWORK 13B

Example   Solve the equation $3x - 5 = 16$ by 'doing the same to both sides'.

$$3x - 5 = 16 \qquad \text{Add 5 to both sides}$$
$$3x - 5 + 5 = 16 + 5$$
$$3x = 21 \qquad \text{Divide both sides by 3}$$
$$\frac{3x}{3} = \frac{21}{3}$$
$$x = 7$$

Solve each of the following equations by 'doing the same to both sides'. Do not forget to check that each answer works in the original equation.

1 $x + 5 = 6$ **2** $y - 3 = 4$ **3** $x + 5 = 3$ **4** $2y + 4 = 12$

5 $3t + 5 = 20$ **6** $2x - 4 = 12$ **7** $6b + 3 = 21$ **8** $4x + 1 = 5$

9 $2m - 3 = 4$ **10** $\dfrac{x}{2} - 5 = 2$ **11** $\dfrac{a}{3} + 3 = 6$ **12** $\dfrac{z}{5} - 1 = 1$

HOMEWORK 13C

Example   Solve $4x + 3 = 23$

Subtract 3 to give $4x = 23 - 3 = 20$
Now divide both sides by 4 to give $x = 20 \div 4 = 5$
The solution is $x = 5$

Solve each of the following equations. Do not forget to check that each answer works in the original equation.

1 $2x + 1 = 7$	**2** $2t + 5 = 13$	**3** $3x + 5 = 17$	**4** $4y + 7 = 27$
5 $2x - 8 = 12$	**6** $5t - 3 = 27$	**7** $\frac{x}{2} + 3 = 6$	**8** $\frac{p}{3} + 2 = 3$
9 $\frac{x}{2} - 3 = 5$	**10** $8 - x = 2$	**11** $13 - 2k = 3$	**12** $6 - 3z = 0$

HOMEWORK 13D

Example   Solve $3(2x - 7) = 15$

First multiply out the bracket to get
$6x - 21 = 15$ Add 21 to both sides
$6x = 36$ Divide both sides by 6
$x = 6$

Solve each of the following equations. Some of the answers may be decimals or negative numbers. Remember to check that each answer works in the original equation. Use your calculator if necessary.

1 $2(x + 1) = 8$	**2** $3(x - 3) = 12$	**3** $3(t + 2) = 9$	**4** $2(x + 5) = 20$
5 $2(2y - 5) = 14$	**6** $2(3x + 4) = 26$	**7** $4(3t - 1) = 20$	**8** $2(t + 5) = 6$
9 $2(x + 4) = 2$	**10** $2(3y - 2) = 5$	**11** $4(3k - 1) = 11$	**12** $5(2x + 3) = 26$

HOMEWORK 13E

Example   Solve $5x + 4 = 3x + 10$

Subtract $3x$ from both sides	$2x + 4 = 10$
Subtract 4 from both sides	$2x = 6$
Divide both sides by 2	$x = 3$

Solve each of the following equations.

1 $2x + 1 = x + 3$	**2** $3y + 2 = 2y + 6$	**3** $5a - 3 = 4a + 4$
4 $5t + 3 = 3t + 9$	**5** $7p - 5 = 5p + 3$	**6** $6k + 5 = 3k + 20$
7 $6m + 1 = m + 11$	**8** $5s - 1 = 2s - 7$	**9** $4w + 8 = 2w + 8$
10 $5x + 5 = 3x + 10$	**11** $5(t - 2) = 4t - 1$	**12** $4(x + 2) = 2(x + 1)$

HOMEWORK 13F

Set up an equation to represent each situation described below. Then solve the equation. Do not forget to check each answer.

1   A girl is Y years old. Her father is 23 years older than she is. The sum of their ages is 37. How old is the girl?

2   A boy is X years old. His sister is twice as old as he is. The sum of their ages is 24. How old is the boy?

3   The diagram shows a rectangle.
Find x if the perimeter is 24 cm.

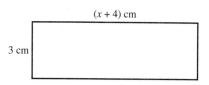

4   Find the length of each side of the pentagon,
if it has a perimeter of 32 cm.

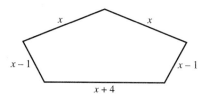

5   On a bookshelf there are $2b$ crime novels, $3b - 2$ science fiction novels and $b + 7$ romance novels. Find how many of each type of book there is, if there are 65 books altogether.

★6   Maureen thought of a number. She multiplied it by 4 and then added 6 to get an answer of 26. What number did she start with?

★7   Declan also thought of a number. He took away 4 from the number and then multiplied by 3 to get an answer of 24. What number did he start with?

★8   Sandeep's money box contains 50p coins, £1 coins and £2 coins.
In the box there are twice as many £1 coins than 50p coins and 4 more £2 coins than 50p coins. There are 44 coins in the box.
   a   Find the how many of each coin there is in the box.
   b   How much money does Sandeep have in her money box?

Chapter 14   Graphs

HOMEWORK 14A

1   A hire firm hired out large scanners. They used the following graph to approximate what the charges would be.

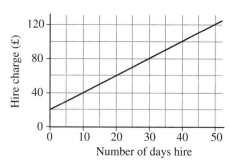

   a   Use the graph to find the approximate charge for hiring a scanner for
      i   20 days   **ii**   30 days   **iii**   50 days
   b   Use the graph to find out how many days hire you would get for a cost of
      i   £120   **ii**   £100   **iii**   £70

2 A conference centre used the following chart for the approximate cost of a conference based on the number of people attending it.

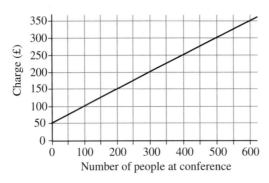

a Use the graph to find the approximate charge for
   i 500 people   **ii** 300 people   **iii** 250 people.

b Use the graph to estimate how many people can attend a conference at the centre for a cost of
   i £250   **ii** £150   **iii** £125

3 Jayne lost her fuel bill, but while talking to her friends, she found out that:
    Kris who had used 750 units was charged £69
    Nic who had used 250 units was charged £33
    Shami who had used 500 units was charged £51

a Plot the given information and draw a straight-line graph. Use a scale from 0 to 800 on the horizontal units axis, and from £0 to £70 on the vertical cost axis.

b Use your graph to find what Jayne will be charged for 420 units.

HOMEWORK 14B

1 Joe was travelling in his car to meet his girlfriend. He set off from home at 9.00 pm, and stopped on the way for a break. This distance–time graph illustrates his journey.

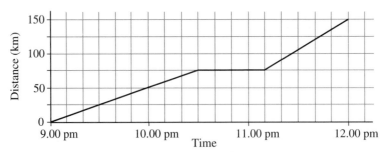

a At what time did he
   i stop for his break   **ii** set off after his break   **iii** get to his meeting place?

b At what average speed was he travelling
   i over the first hour   **ii** over the last hour   **iii** for the whole of his journey?

2 A taxi set off from Hellaby to pick up Jean. It then went on to pick up Jeans's parents. It then travelled further, dropping them all off at a shopping centre. The taxi went on a further 10 km to pick up another party and took them back to Hellaby. This distance–time graph illustrates the journey.

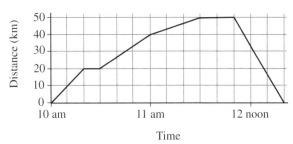

a How far from Hellaby did Jean's parents live?
b How far from Hellaby is the shopping centre?
c What was the average speed of the taxi while only Jean was in the taxi?
d What was the average speed of the taxi back to Hellaby?

3 Grandad took his grandchildren out for a trip. He set off at 1.00 pm and travelled, for half an hour, away from Norwich at an average speed of 60 km/h. They stopped to look at the sea and have an ice cream. At two o'clock, they set off again, travelling for a quarter of an hour at an average speed of 80 km/h. Then they stopped to play on the sand for half an hour. Grandad then drove the grandchildren back home at an average speed of 50 km/h. Draw a travel graph to illustrate this story. Use a horizontal axis to represent time from 1 pm to 4 pm, and a vertical scale from 0 km to 50 km.

HOMEWORK 14C

1 Draw the graph of $y = x + 1$

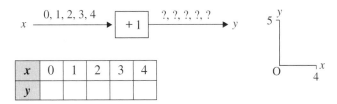

2 Draw the graph of $y = 2x + 1$

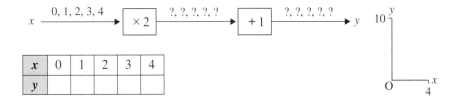

3 Draw the graph of $y = 3x + 1$

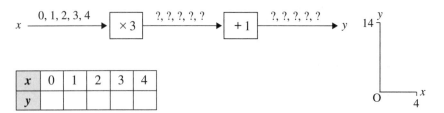

x	0	1	2	3	4
y					

4 Draw the graph of $y = x - 1$

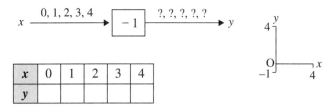

x	0	1	2	3	4
y					

★**5** **a** Draw the graphs of $y = x - 2$ and $y = 2x - 1$ on the same grid.
    b Where do the graphs cross?

★**6** **a** Draw the graphs of $y = 2x$ and $y = x + 2$ on the same grid
    b Where do the graphs cross?

HOMEWORK 14D

Draw the graph for each of the equations given.

Follow these hints.
- Use the highest and smallest values of x given as your range.
- When the first part of the function is a division, pick x-values that divide exactly to avoid fractions.
- Always label your graphs. This is particularly important when you are drawing two graphs on the same set of axes.
- Create a table of values. You will often have to complete these in your examinations.

1 Draw the graph of $y = 2x + 3$ for x-values from 0 to 5 ($0 \leq x \leq 5$)

2 Draw the graph of $y = 3x - 1$ ($0 \leq x \leq 5$)

3 Draw the graph of $y = \dfrac{x}{2} - 2$ ($0 \leq x \leq 12$)

4 Draw the graph of $y = 2x + 1$ ($-2 \leq x \leq 2$)

5 Draw the graph of $y = \dfrac{x}{2} + 5$ ($-6 \leq x \leq 6$)

6 **a** On the same set of axes, draw the graphs of
    $y = 3x - 1$ and $y = 2x + 3$ ($0 \leq x \leq 5$)
    b Where do the two graphs cross?

7 **a** On the same axes, draw the graphs of
    $y = 4x - 3$ and $y = 3x + 2$ ($0 \leq x \leq 6$)
    b Where do the two graphs cross?

8 **a** On the same axes, draw the graphs of

$y = \dfrac{x}{2} + 1$ and $y = \dfrac{x}{3} + 2$ $(0 \leq x \leq 12)$

  b Where do the two graphs cross?

9 **a** On the same axes, draw the graphs of
$y = 2x + 3$ and $y = 2x - 1$ $(0 \leq x \leq 4)$

  b Do the graphs cross? If not, why not?

10 **a** Copy and complete the table to draw the graph of
$x + y = 6$ $(0 \leq x \leq 6)$

  b Now draw the graph of $x + y = 3$

x	0	1	2	3	4	5	6
y							

Chapter 15   Angles

HOMEWORK 15A

1 Use a protractor to find the size of each marked angle.

  a
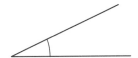

  b

  c

  d

  e

  f

  g

  h

2 Draw angles of the following sizes.
   a 30°   **b** 42°   **c** 55°   **d** 68°   **e** 75°   **f** 140°
   g 164°   **h** 245°

3 **a** Draw any three acute angles.
   b Estimate their sizes. Record your results.
   c Measure the angles. Record your results.
   d Work out the difference between your estimate and your measurement for each angle.

Calculate the size of the angle marked with a letter in each of these examples.

1

2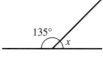

3

4

5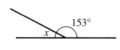

6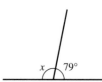

7

8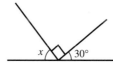

9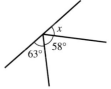

10

11

12

Example Find the value of x in the diagram.

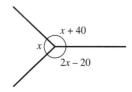

These angles are around a point and add up to 360°.

So $x + x + 40 + 2x - 20 = 360°$

$$4x + 20 = 360°$$
$$4x = 340°$$
$$x = 85°$$

1 Calculate the value of x in each of these examples.

a

b

c

2 Calculate the value of x in each of these examples.

a

b

c

3 Calculate the value of x first and then find the size of angle y in each of these examples.

a

b

c

HOMEWORK 15D

1 Find the size of the angle marked with a letter in each of these triangles.

a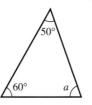

b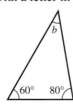

c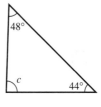

d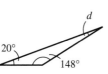

e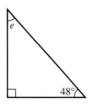

f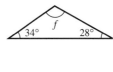

2 Are any of these sets of angles the three angles of a triangle? Explain your answer.
   a 15°, 85° and 80°   **b** 40°, 60° and 90°   **c** 25°, 25° and 110°
   d 40°, 40° and 100°   **e** 32°, 37° and 111°   **f** 61°, 59° and 70°

3 The three interior angles of a triangle are given in each case. Find the angle indicated by a letter.
   a 40°, 70° and $a°$ **b** 60°, 60° and $b°$ **c** 80°, 90° and $c°$
   d 65°, 72° and $d°$ **e** 130°, 45° and $e°$ **f** 112°, 27° and $f°$

4 In a triangle all the interior angles are the same.
   a What size is each angle?
   b What is the special name of this triangle?
   c What is special about the sides of this triangle?

5 In the triangle on the right, two of the angles are the same.

  a Work out the size of the lettered angles.

  b What is the special name of a triangle like this?

  c What is special about the sides AB and AC of this triangle?

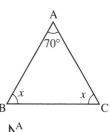

6 In the triangle on the right, the size of the angle at C is twice the size of the angle at A. Work out the size of the lettered angles.

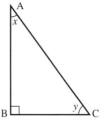

★7 Find the size of the angle marked with a letter in each of the diagrams.

a

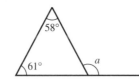

b

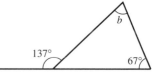

🖉 HOMEWORK 15E

1 Find the size of the angle marked with a letter in each of these quadrilaterals.

a

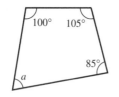

b

c

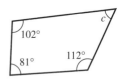

d

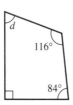

e

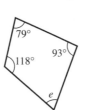

f

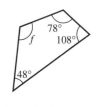

2 Are any of these sets of angles the four interior angles of a quadrilateral? Explain your answer.

  a 125°, 65°, 70° and 90°

  b 100°, 60°, 70° and 130°

  c 85°, 95°, 85° and 95°

  d 120°, 120°, 70° and 60°

  e 112°, 68°, 32° and 138°

  f 151°, 102°, 73° and 34°

3 Three interior angles of a quadrilateral are given. Find the one indicated by a letter.

  a 110°, 90°, 70° and $a°$

  b 100°, 100°, 80° and $b°$

  c 60°, 60°, 160° and $c°$

  d 135°, 122°, 57° and $d°$

  e 125°, 142°, 63° and $e°$

  f 102°, 72°, 49° and $f°$

★**4** For the quadrilateral on the right
  a Find the size of angle x.
  b What type of angle is x?
  c What is the special name of a
    quadrilateral like this?

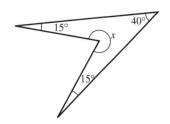

1 For each regular polygon below, find the interior angle x and the exterior angle y.

a 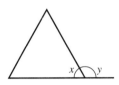 **b** 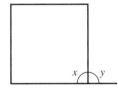 **c**

d  **e**

2 a Draw a diagram to explain why the sum of the interior angles of any pentagon is 540°.
  b Find the size of the angle x in the pentagon.

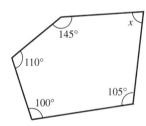

3 Explain why an exterior angle of a regular polygon cannot be 25°.

1 State the size of the lettered angles in each diagram.

a 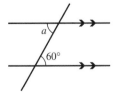 **b** 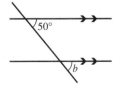 **c**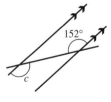

d 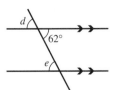 **e** 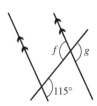 **f**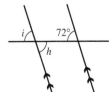

2 State the size of the lettered angles in each diagram.

a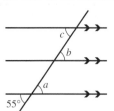

b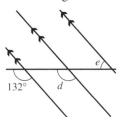

c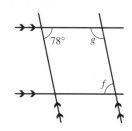

3 State the size of the lettered angles in these diagrams.

a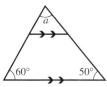

b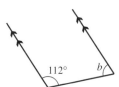

✎ HOMEWORK 15H

1 For each of these trapeziums, calculate the sizes of the lettered angles.

a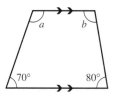

b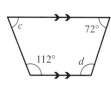

c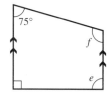

2 For each of these parallelograms, calculate the sizes of the lettered angles.

a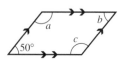

b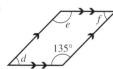

c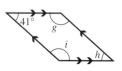

3 For each of these kites, calculate the sizes of the lettered angles.

a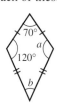

b

c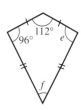

4 For each of these rhombuses, calculate the sizes of the lettered angles.

a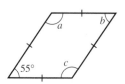

b

c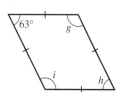

1 a Write down the bearing of B from A   **b** Write down the bearing of D from C.

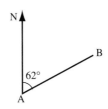

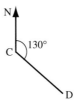

c Write down the bearing of F from E.   **d** Write down the bearing of H from G.

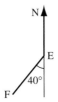

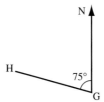

★**2** Look at the map of Britain.
By measuring angles, find the bearing of
a London from Edinburgh
b London from Cardiff
c Edinburgh from Cardiff
d Cardiff from London

HOMEWORK 16A

Example   Calculate the circumference of the circle with a diameter of 4 cm.

Use the formula $c = \pi d$. So $c = \pi \times 4 = 12.6$ cm (1dp)

1   Calculate the circumference of each circle illustrated below.
Give your answers to one decimal place.

a 3 cm

b 9 cm

c 10cm

d 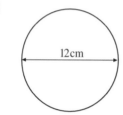 12cm

e 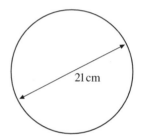 21cm

2   Calculate the circumference of each circle illustrated below.
Give your answers to one decimal place.

a 2 cm

b 3.5 cm

c 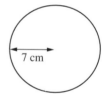 7 cm

d 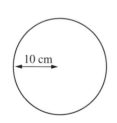 10 cm

e  12.5 cm

★**3**   A fence is to be put around a circular pond which has a diameter of 15 m. What is the length of fencing required, if the fencing is bought in 1 m lengths?

★**4**   Roger trains for an athletics competition by running round a circular track which has a radius of 50 m.
   a   Calculate the circumference of the track. Give your answer to 1 decimal place.
   b   How many complete circuits will he need to run to be sure of running 5000 m?

5 Calculate the perimeter of this semicircle.

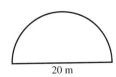

20 m

6 What is the diameter of a circle whose circumference is 40 cm? Give your answer to one decimal place.

◯ HOMEWORK 16B

Example Calculate the area of a circle with a radius of 7 cm.

Use the formula $A = \pi r^2$. So $A = \pi \times r \times r = \pi \times 7 \times 7 = 153.9 \text{ cm}^2$ (1 dp)

1 Calculate the area of each circle illustrated below. Give your answers to one decimal place.

a 2 cm

b 6 cm

c 8 cm

d 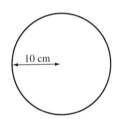 10 cm

e 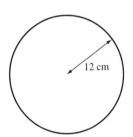 12 cm

2 Calculate the area of each circle illustrated below. Give your answers to one decimal place.

a 2 cm

b 6 cm

c 10 cm

d 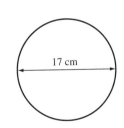 17 cm

e 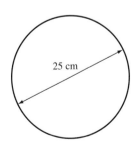 25 cm

★**3** A circular table has a diameter of 80 cm.
  a Calculate the circumference of the table, giving your answer in metres to 1 decimal place.
  b Calculate the area of the table, giving your answer in square metres to 1 decimal place.

★4 The diagram shows a circular path around a flower bed in a park. The radius of the flower bed is 6 m and the width of the path is 1 m.

  a Calculate the area of the flower bed.
  b Write down the radius of the large circle.
  c Calculate the area of the large circle.
  d Calculate the area of the path.

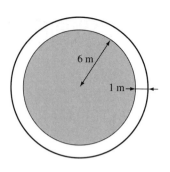

5 The diagram shows a running track.

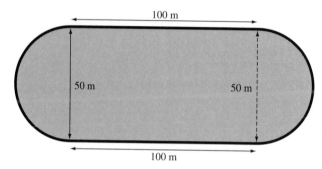

  a Calculate the perimeter of the track.
  b Calculate the total area inside the track.

6 A circle has a circumference of 50 cm.

  a Calculate the diameter of the circle to one decimal place.
  b What is the radius of the circle to one decimal place?
  c Calculate the area of the circle to one decimal place.

HOMEWORK 16C

Find the volume of each 3-D shape if the edge of each cube is 1 cm.

1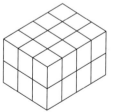

2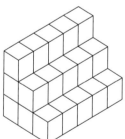

3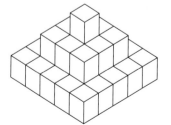

4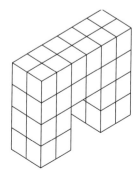

Example   Calculate the volume and surface area of this cuboid.

$$\text{Volume} = 6 \times 4 \times 3.5 = 84\,\text{cm}^3$$
$$\text{Surface area} = (2 \times 6 \times 4) + (2 \times 3.5 \times 4) +$$
$$(2 \times 3.5 \times 6)$$
$$= 48 + 28 + 42 = 118\,\text{cm}^2$$

4 cm

3.5 cm

6 cm

1   Find **i** the volume and **ii** the surface area of each of these cuboids.

a

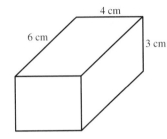

4 cm
6 cm
3 cm

b

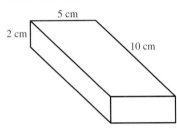

5 cm
2 cm
10 cm

c

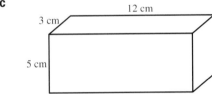

12 cm
3 cm
5 cm

d

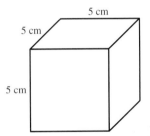

5 cm
5 cm
5 cm
5 cm

2   Copy and complete the table which shows the dimensions and volumes of four cuboids.

Length	Width	Height	Volume
4 cm	3 cm	2 cm	
	3 cm	3 cm	45 cm³
8 cm		4 cm	160 cm³
6 cm	6 cm		216 cm³

3   Find the capacity (volume of a liquid or a gas) of a swimming pool whose dimensions are: length 12 m, width 5 m and depth 1.5 m.

4   Find the volume of the cuboid in each of the following cases.
  a   The area of the base is 20 cm² and the height is 3 cm.
  b   The base has one side 4 cm, the other side 1 cm longer, and the height is 8 cm.
  c   The area of the top is 40 cm² and the depth is 3 cm.

★5 How many 'stock-cubes' will fit into the box?

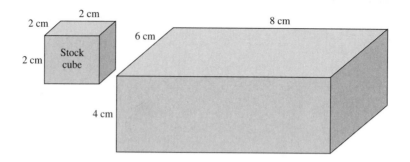

6 Calculate the volume of each of these shapes.

a

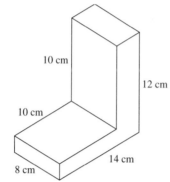

b

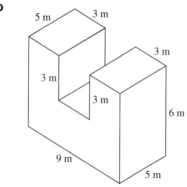

HOMEWORK 17A

1 Measure the radius of each of the following circles, giving your answers in centimetres. Write down the diameter of each circle.

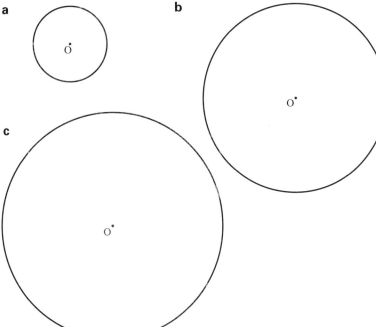

a

b

c

2 Draw circles with the following measurements.

   a Radius = 1.5 cm   **b** Radius = 4 cm

   c Diameter = 7 cm   **d** Diameter = 9.6 cm

3 Accurately draw the following shapes.

   a

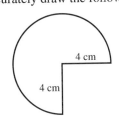

4 cm

4 cm

   b

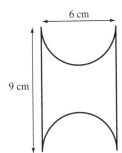

6 cm

9 cm

4 Draw an accurate copy of this diagram. What is the length of the diameter of the circle?

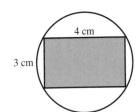

4 cm

3 cm

5 Draw an accurate copy of this diagram at full scale.
What is the diameter of the circle?

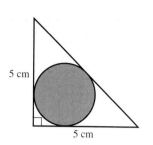

5 cm

5 cm

Q HOMEWORK 17B

1 Accurately draw each of the following triangles.

a

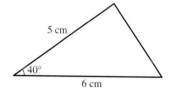

5 cm

6 cm

40°

b

75°

55°

5 cm

c

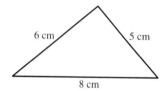

6 cm

5 cm

8 cm

d

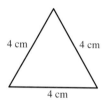

4 cm

4 cm

4 cm

e

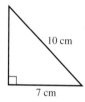

10 cm

7 cm

2 Draw a triangle ABC with AB = 6 cm, ∠A = 60° and ∠B = 50°.

3

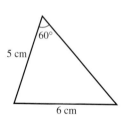

60°

5 cm

6 cm

Explain why you can or cannot draw this triangle accurately.

4 **a** Accurately draw the shape on the right.
b What is the name of the shape you have drawn?

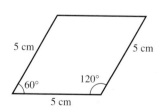

5 cm

5 cm

60°

120°

5 cm

1 State whether each pair of shapes **a** to **f** are congruent or not.

a 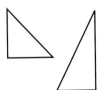 **b** 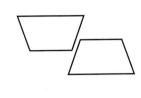 **c**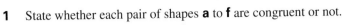

d 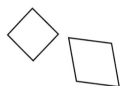 **e** 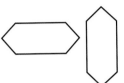 **f**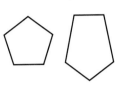

2 Which figure in each group of shapes is not congruent to the other two?

a

1   2   3

b

1   2   3

c

1   2   3

d

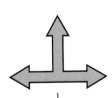 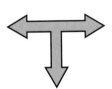 

1   2   3

Chapter 18 Probability

HOMEWORK 18A

1   When throwing a fair dice, state whether each of the following events are impossible, very unlikely, unlikely, evens, likely, very likely or certain.
   a   The score is a factor of 20.
   b   The score is $3\frac{1}{2}$
   c   The score is a number less than six.
   d   The score is a one.
   e   The score is a number greater than zero.
   f   The score is an odd number.
   g   The score is a multiple of three.

2   Draw a probability scale and put an arrow to show approximately the probability of each of the following events happening.
   a   It will snow on Christmas Day this year.
   b   The sun will rise tomorrow morning.
   c   Someone in your class will have a birthday this month.
   d   It will rain tomorrow.
   e   Someone will win the Jackpot in the National Lottery this week.

3   Give an event of your own where you think the probability is:
   a   impossible   b   very unlikely   c   unlikely   d   evens
   e   likely   f   very likely   g   certain

HOMEWORK 18B

Example   A bag contains 5 red balls and 3 blue balls. A ball is taken out at random. What is the probability that it is: **a** red   **b** blue   **c** green?

   a   There are 5 red balls out of a total of 8, so P(red) = $\frac{5}{8}$
   b   There are 3 blue balls out of a total of 8, so P(blue) = $\frac{3}{8}$
   c   There are no green balls, so this event is impossible: P(green) = 0

1   When drawing a card from a well shuffled pack of cards, what is the probability of each of the following events? Remember to cancel down the probability fraction if possible.
   a   Drawing an Ace.   b   Drawing a picture card.
   c   Drawing a Diamond.   d   Drawing a Queen or a King.
   e   Drawing the Ace of Spades.   f   Drawing a red Jack.
   g   Drawing a Club or a Heart.

2   The numbers 1 to 10 inclusive are placed in a hat. Irene takes a number out of the bag without looking. What is the probability that she draws
   a   the number 10   b   an odd number
   c   a number greater than 4   d   a prime number
   e   a number between 5 and 9?

3 A bag contains 2 blue balls, 3 red balls and 4 green balls. Frank takes a ball from the bag without looking. What is the probability that he takes out

    a a blue ball   **b** a red ball   **c** a ball that is not green   **d** a yellow ball?

4 In a prize raffle there are 50 tickets: 10 coloured red, 10 coloured blue and the rest coloured white. What is the probability that the first ticket drawn out is

    a red   **b** blue   **c** white   **d** red or white   **e** not blue?

5 A bag contains 15 coloured balls. Three are red, five are blue and the rest are black. Paul takes a ball at random from the bag.

    a Find

        i P (he chooses a red)   **ii** P (he chooses a blue)   **iii** P(he chooses a black)

    b Add together the three probabilities. What do you notice?

    c Explain your answer to part **b**.

6 Boris knows that when he plays a game of chess, he has a 65% chance of winning a game and a 15% chance of losing a game. What is the probability that he draws a game?

HOMEWORK 18C

Example   What is the probability of not picking an Ace from a pack of cards?

        First, find the probability of picking an Ace: P (picking an Ace) $= \frac{4}{52} = \frac{1}{13}$

        Therefore, P (not picking an Ace) $= 1 - \frac{1}{13} = \frac{12}{13}$

1 **a** The probability of winning a prize in a tombola is $\frac{1}{20}$. What is the probability of not winning a prize in the tombola?

    b The probability that it will rain tomorrow is 65%. What is the probability that it will not rain tomorrow?

    c The probability that Josie wins a game of tennis is 0.8, what is the probability that she loses a game?

    d The probability of getting a double six when throwing two dice is $\frac{1}{36}$. What is the probability of not getting a double six?

2 Harvinder picks a card from a pack of well-shuffled playing cards. Find the probability that she picks:

    a i a King   **ii** a card that is not a King

    b i a Spade   **ii** a card that is not a Spade

    c i a 9 or a 10   **ii** neither a 9 nor a 10.

★3 The following letters are put into a bag.

    a Stan takes a letter at random. What is the probability that

        i he takes a letter A   **ii** he does not take a letter A?

    b Pat takes an R and keeps it. Stan now takes a letter from those remaining.

        i What is the probability that he takes a letter A?

        ii What is the probability that he does not take a letter A?

1 Katrina throws two dice and records the number of doubles that she gets after various numbers of throws. The table shows her results.

Number of throws	10	20	30	50	100	200	600
Number of doubles	2	3	6	9	17	35	102

   a Calculate the experimental probability of a double at each stage that Katrina recorded her results.

   b What do you think the theoretical probability is for the number of doubles when throwing two dice?

2 Mary made a six-sided spinner, like the one shown in the diagram. She used it to play a board game with her friend Jane. The girls thought that the spinner wasn't very fair as it seemed to land on some numbers more than others. They threw the spinner 120 times and recorded the results. The results are shown in the table.

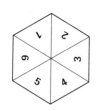

Number spinner lands on	1	2	3	4	5	6
Number of times	22	17	21	18	26	16

   a Work out the experimental probability of each number.

   b How many times would you expect each number to occur if the spinner is fair?

   c Do you think that the spinner is fair? Give a reason for your answer.

3 In a game at the fair-ground a player rolls a coin onto a squared board with some of the squares coloured blue, green or red. If the coin lands completely within one of the coloured squares the player wins a prize. The table below shows the probabilities of the coin landing completely within a winning colour.

Colour	Blue	Green	Red
Probability	0.3	0.2	0.1

   a On one afternoon 300 games were played. How many coins would you expect to land within **i** a blue square **ii** a green square **iii** a red square?

   b What is the probability that a player loses a game?

1 Copy and complete the sample space diagram to show the total score when two dice are thrown together.

   a What is the most likely score?

   b Which two scores are least likely?

   c Write down the probability of getting a double six.

   d What is the probability that a score is

      i 11 **ii** 4 **iii** greater than 9

      iv an odd number **v** 4 or less

      vi a multiple of 4?

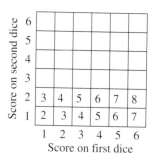

2 Copy and complete the sample space diagram to show the outcomes when a dice and a coin are thrown together.

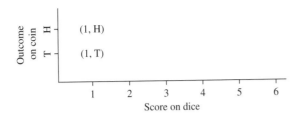

Find the probability of getting

a a Head and a score of 6

b a Tail and an even score

c a score of 3.

★**3** Elaine throws a coin and spins a 5-sided spinner. One possible outcome is (Heads, 5).

a List all the possible outcomes.

b What is the probability of getting Tails on the coin and an odd number on the spinner?

★**4** A bag contains five discs that are numbered 2, 4, 6, 8 and 10. Sharleen takes a disc at random from the bag and puts the disc back. She shakes the bag and takes a disc again. She adds together the two numbers on the discs she has chosen.

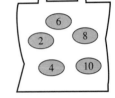

a Copy and complete the table to show all the possible totals.

First number

Second number	2	4	6	8	10
2					
4					
6					
8					
10					

b Find the probability that the total is

i 12 **ii** 20 **iii** 15 **iv** a square number **v** a multiple of 3.

HOMEWORK 19A

1 Copy each of these shapes on squared paper and draw its image by using the given translation.

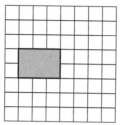

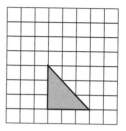

a 4 squares right   **b** 4 squares up

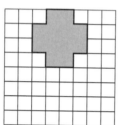

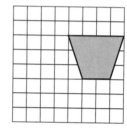

c 4 squares down   **d** 4 squares left

2 Copy each of these shapes on squared paper and draw its image by using the given translation.

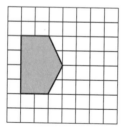

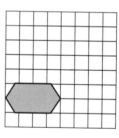

a 3 squares right and 2 squares down   **b** 3 squares right and 4 squares up

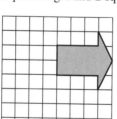

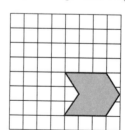

c 3 squares left and 3 squares down   **d** 4 squares left and 1 square up

3 Look at the diagram below, then describe these translations.

a **i** A to B   **ii** A to C   **iii** A to D   **iv** A to E
b **i** B to A   **ii** B to C   **iii** B to D   **iv** B to E
c **i** C to A   **ii** C to B   **iii** C to D   **iv** C to E
d **i** D to E   **ii** E to B   **iii** D to C   **iv** E to D

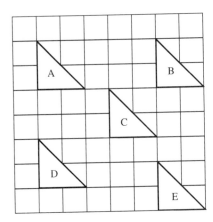

4 Draw a rectangle whose vertices have coordinates A(1, 1), B(4, 1), C(4, 3) and D(1, 3). Translate the rectangle 5 squares right and 4 squares up to form the image rectangle A′B′C′D′. Write down the coordinates of A′, B′, C′ and D′.

HOMEWORK 19B

1 Copy each shape on squared paper and draw its image after a reflection in the given mirror line.

a

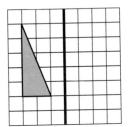

b

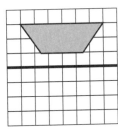

c

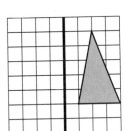

d

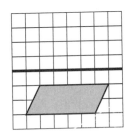

2 Draw each of these figures on squared paper and then draw the reflection of the figure in the mirror line.

a
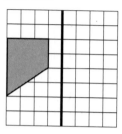

b
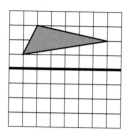

c
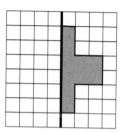

d
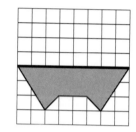

★3 Copy this diagram on squared paper.

a Reflect the triangle ABC in the x-axis. Label the image R.

b Reflect the triangle ABC in the y-axis. Label the image S.

c What special name is given to figures that are exactly the same shape and size?

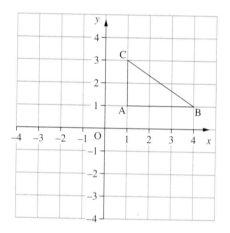

4 **a** Draw a pair of axes with the x-axis from –5 to 5 and the y-axis from –5 to 5.

   b Draw the triangle with coordinates A(1, 1), B(5, 5), C(3, 4).

   c Reflect triangle ABC in the x-axis. Label the image P.

   d Reflect triangle P in the y-axis. Label the image Q.

   e Reflect triangle Q in the x-axis. Label the image R.

   f Describe the reflection that will transform triangle ABC onto triangle R.

1 Copy each of these diagrams on squared paper. Draw its image using the given rotation about the centre of rotation A. Using tracing paper may help.

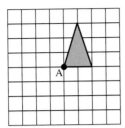

a ½ turn

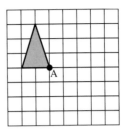

b ¼ turn clockwise

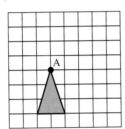

c ¼ turn anticlockwise

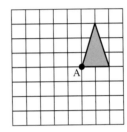

d ¾ turn turn clockwise

2 Copy each of these flags on squared paper. Draw its image using the given rotation about the centre of rotation A. Using tracing paper may help.

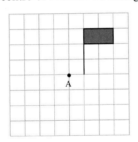

a 180° turn

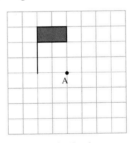

b 90° turn clockwise

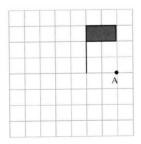

c 90° turn anticlockwise

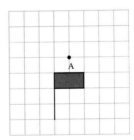

d 270° turn clockwise

★3 Copy this T-shape on squared paper.

    a Rotate the shape 90° clockwise about the origin O. Label the image P.

    b Rotate the shape 180° clockwise about the origin O. Label the image Q.

    c Rotate the shape 270° clockwise about the origin O. Label the image R.

    d What rotation takes R back to the original shape?

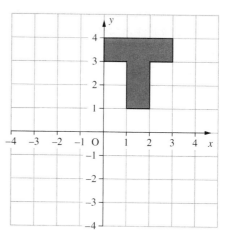

★4 Copy this square ABCD on squared paper.

    a Write down the coordinates of the vertices of the square ABCD.

    b Rotate the square ABCD through 90° clockwise about the origin O. Label the image S. Write down the coordinates of the vertices of the square S.

    c Rotate the square ABCD through 180° clockwise about the origin O. Label the image T. Write down the coordinates of the vertices of the square T.

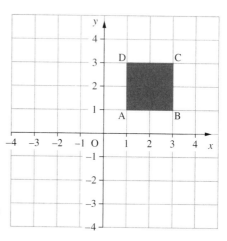

    d Rotate the square ABCD through 270° clockwise about the origin O. Label the image U. Write down the coordinates of the vertices of the square U.

    e What do you notice about the coordinates of the four squares?

HOMEWORK 19D

1 Copy each of these figures onto squared paper with its centre of enlargement A. Then enlarge it by the given scale factor, using the ray method.

    a

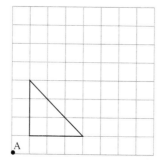

Scale factor 2

    b

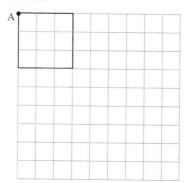

Scale factor 3

2 Copy each of these diagrams on squared paper and enlarge it by scale factor 2, using the origin as the centre of enlargement.

a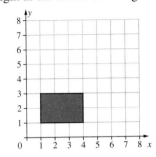

b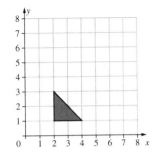

c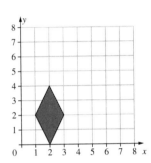

d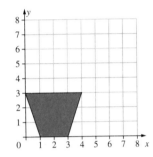

HOMEWORK 19E

1 On squared paper, show how each of these shapes tessellate. You should draw at least 6 shapes.

a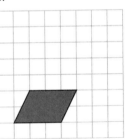

b

c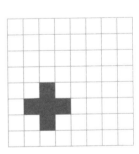

d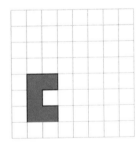

2 Use isometric paper to show how a regular hexagon tessellates.

HOMEWORK 20A

1   The grid below shows the floor plan of a kitchen. The scale is 1 cm to 30 cm.

Work space			Cooker			Work space		
Sink Unit								Fridge
				Cupboards				Door
Door								

a   State the actual dimensions of
i   the sink unit   **ii**   the cooker   **iii**   the fridge   **iv**   the cupboards.

b   Calculate the actual total area of the work space.

★**2**   On the right is a sketch of a ladder leaning against a wall.
The bottom of the ladder is 1 m away from the wall and it reaches
4 m up the wall.

a   Make a scale drawing to show the position of the ladder. Use a
scale of 4 cm to 1 m.

b   Use your scale drawing to work out the actual length of the
ladder.

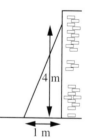

4 m

1 m

3 The map below is drawn to a scale of 1 cm to 2 km.

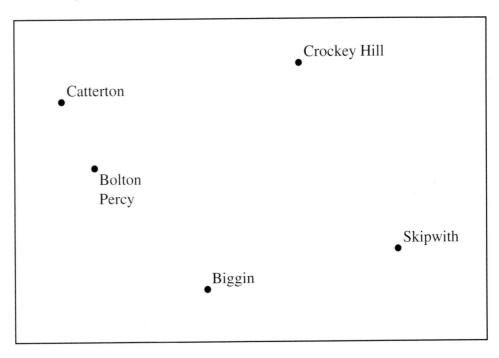

Find the distances between

  a Biggin and Skipwith   **b** Bolton Percy and Crockey Hill

  c Skipwith and Catterton   **d** Crockey Hill and Biggin

  e Catterton and Bolton Percy.

4 The map below shows the position of four fells in the Lake District. The map is drawn to a scale of 1 : 150 000.

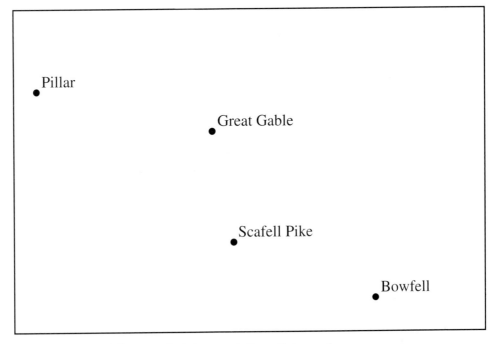

To the nearest kilometre, find the actual direct distances from:

  a Scafell Pike to Great Gable   **b** Scafell Pike to Pillar

  c Great Gable to Pillar   **d** Pillar to Bowfell

  e Bowfell to Great Gable.

1 Four nets are shown below. Copy the nets which would make a cube.

a

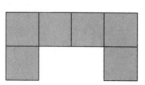

b

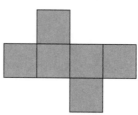

c

d

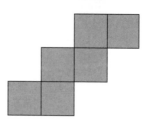

2 Draw, on squared paper, an accurate net for each of these cuboids.

a

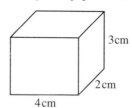

b

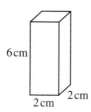

3 Draw an accurate net for this triangular prism.

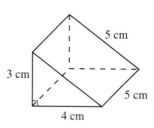

★**4** The diagram shows a sketch of a square-based pyramid.

    a Write down how many

       i vertices

       ii edges

       iii faces the pyramid has.

    b Draw an accurate net for the pyramid.

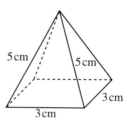

1 Draw accurately each of these cuboids on an isometric grid.

a

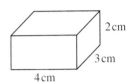

b

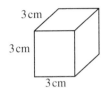

2 Draw accurately each of these 3-D shapes on an isometric grid.

a

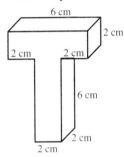

b

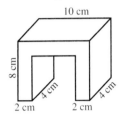

3 For each of the following 3-D shapes, draw on squared paper

    i the plan   **ii** the front elevation   **iii** the side elevation.

a

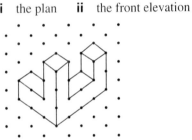

b

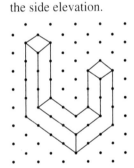

Chapter 21   Units

Decide in which metric unit you would most likely measure each of the following amounts.

1 The height of your best friend.

2 The distance from School to your home.

3 The thickness of a CD.

4 The weight of your maths teacher.

5 The amount of water in a lake.

6 The weight of a slice of bread.

7 The length of a double decker bus

8 The weight of a kitten

Estimate the approximate metric length, weight or capacity of each of the following.

9 This book (both length and weight).

10 The length of the road you live on. (You do not need to walk along it all.)

11 The capacity of a bottle of wine (metric measure).

12 A door (length, width and weight).

13 The diameter of a £1 coin, and its weight.

14 The distance from your school to The Houses of Parliamant (London).

HOMEWORK 21B

Length	10 mm = 1 cm, 1000 mm = 100 cm = 1 m, 1000 m = 1 km
Weight	1000 gm = 1 kg , 1000 kg = 1 t
Capacity	10 ml = 1 cl, 1000 ml = 100 cl = 1 litre
Volume	1000 litres = 1 m³, 1 ml = 1 cm³

Fill in the gaps using the information above.

1 155 cm = ... m
2 95 mm = ... cm
3 780 mm = ... m
4 3100 m = ... km
5 310 cm = ... m
6 3050 mm = ... m
7 156 mm = ... cm
8 2180 m = ... km
9 1070 mm = ... m
10 1324 cm = ... m
11 175 m = ... km
12 83 mm = ... m
13 620 mm = ... cm
14 2130 cm = ... m
15 5120 m = ... km
16 8150 g = ... kg
17 2300 kg = ... t
18 32 ml = ... cl
19 1360 ml = ... l
20 580 cl = ... l
21 950 kg = ... t
22 120 g = ... kg
23 150 ml = ... l
24 350 cl = ... l
25 540 ml = ... cl
26 2060 kg = ... t
27 7500 ml = ... l
28 3800 g = ... kg
29 605 cl = ... l
30 15 ml = ... l
31 6300 l = ... m³
32 45 ml = ... cm³
33 2350 l = ... m³
34 720 l = ... m³
35 8.2 m = ... cm
36 71 km = ... m
37 8.6 m = ... mm
38 15.6 cm = ... mm
39 0.83 m = ... cm
40 5.15 km = ... m
41 1.85 cm = ... mm
42 2.75 m = ... cm

HOMEWORK 21C

Length	12 inches = 1 foot, 3 feet = 1 yard, 1 760 yards = 1 mile
Weight	16 ounces = 1 pound, 14 pounds = 1 stone, 2 240 pounds = 1 ton
Capacity	8 pints = 1 gallon

Fill in the gaps using the information above.

1 5 feet = ... inches
2 5 yards = ... feet
3 3 miles = ... yards
4 6 pounds = ... ounces
5 5 stones = ... pounds
6 2 tons = ... pounds
7 4 gallons = ... pints
8 7 feet = ... inches

9 2 yards = ... inches

10 11 yards = ... feet

11 5 pounds = ... ounces

12 72 inches = ... feet

13 6 stones = ... pounds

14 39 feet = ... yards

15 2 stones = ... ounces

16 4 400 yards = ... miles

17 12 gallons = ... pints

18 2 miles = ... feet

19 84 inches = ... feet

20 105 pounds = ... stones

21 48 pints = ... gallons

22 48 ounces = ... pounds

23 21 feet = ... yards

24 22 400 pounds = ... tons

25 2 miles = ... inches

26 256 ounces = ... pounds

27 80 pints = ... gallons

28 280 pounds = ... stones

29 31680 feet = ... miles

30 2 tons = ... ounces

HOMEWORK 21D

1 kilogram ≈ 2.2 pounds
14 pounds = 1 stone

1 Change each of these weights in kilograms to pounds.
   a 6   **b** 8   **c** 15   **d** 32   **e** 45

2 Change each of these weights in pounds to kilograms. (Give each answer to 1 dp.)
   a 10   **b** 18   **c** 25   **d** 40   **e** 56

3 A boxer weighs in at 176 pounds before a game. What is his weight in kilograms?

4 Martha weighs 8 stones 2 pounds. What is her weight to the nearest kilogram?

5 One hundred-weight is equivalent to 112 pounds. How many kilograms are there in one hundred-weight? Give your answer to 1 dp.

6 Lauren weighs 40 kg and Christine weighs 90 pounds. Who is heavier?

7 Which is heavier: a 12 lb bag of potatoes or a 5 kg bag of potatoes?

8 One parcel weighs 2.4 kg and another parcel weighs 5 lb. Which is the lighter parcel?

HOMEWORK 21E

1 litre ≈ $1\frac{3}{4}$ pints ≈ 1.75 pints

1 Change each of these capacities in litres to pints.
   a 2   **b** 8   **c** 25   **d** 60   **e** 75

2 Change each of these capacities in pints to litres. (Give each answer to the nearest litre.)
   a 7   **b** 20   **c** 35   **d** 42   **e** 100

3 A bucket has a capacity of 10 litres. Danny wants to carry 15 pints of water to make some concrete. Can he do it in one bucketful?

4 There are about 5 litres of blood in an average adult's body. How many pints is this?

5 A fish tank holds 50 *l* of water. How many pints are needed to fill it?

6 A container X holds 45 litres. Container Y holds 80 pints. Which holds less?

7 Oil is sold in 8 pint cans or 5 litre cans. Which can holds more oil?

8 5 pints of milk is the same price as 3 litres of milk. Which is the better buy?

HOMEWORK 21F

8 kilometres ≈ 5 miles

1 Change each of these distances in miles to kilometres.
   a 20   **b** 30   **c** 50   **d** 65   **e** 120

2 Change each of these distances in kilometres to miles.
   a 16   **b** 24   **c** 40   **d** 72   **e** 300

3 This sign indicates the maximum speed limit on a
French motorway in kilometres per hour. What is this speed in
miles per hour?

4 Pierre runs in the London Marathon which covers a distance of just over 26 miles. What is this distance to the nearest kilometre?

5 The table shows the distance, in miles, between four cities in England. Copy the table, without the numbers, and then fill it in with the equivalent distance in kilometres.

Birmingham	120	100	210
	Leeds	75	90
		Liverpool	175
			Newcastle

6 Allan cycles a distance of 42 miles and Wendy cycles a distance of 65 kilometres. Who cycled the greater distance?

7 The direct distance by air from London to Rome is 960 miles and from London to Lisbon is 1600 kilometres. Which is the longer distance?

8 Bill did a 20 mile sponsored walk to raise money for charity and Brian did a 30 kilometre sponsored walk for a different charity. Who walked the greater distance?

HOMEWORK 21G

1 gallon ≈ 4.5 litres

1 Change each of these capacities in gallons to litres.
   a 5   **b** 12   **c** 27   **d** 50   **e** 72

2 Change each of these capacities in litres to gallons.
   a 18   **b** 45   **c** 72   **d** 270   **e** 900

3 A water tank has a capacity of 3200 litres. How many gallons of water can it hold?

4 A 'firkin' is a barrel of beer which holds 9 gallons. How many litres does the barrel hold?

5 Mr Smith puts 76.5 litres of petrol into his car. How many gallons is this?

6 Mr Smith works out that his car does 45 miles to a gallon of petrol. Find the petrol consumption in kilometres per litre.

7 An oil drum has a capacity of 1000 gallons. How many litres of oil can it hold?

8 A reservoir holds 200 million gallons. Water is used at the rate of 10 million litres a day. Assuming that there is a drought and that no water is going into the reservoir, how many days will the store of water last?

HOMEWORK 21H

1 metre ≈ 39 inches
1 foot ≈ 30 cm
1 foot = 12 inches
1 yard = 3 feet

1 Change each of these distances in metres to inches.
   a 2   **b** 5   **c** 8   **d** 10   **e** 12

2 Change each of these distances in feet to centimetres.
   a 3   **b** 5   **c** 7   **d** 10   **e** 30

3 Change each of these distances in inches to metres. (Give your answer to 1 dp.)
   a 48   **b** 52   **c** 60   **d** 75   **e** 100

4 Dylan needs to fill in a form which requires him to state his height in centimetres. He knows that his height is 5 feet 8 inches. Calculate his height in centimetres.

5 The length of a cricket pitch is 22 yards. Work out the length in metres, giving your answer to 2 dp.

6 A mile is 5280 feet. How many metres make a mile? Give your answer to the nearest metre.

7 Which is shallower: a pool with a depth of 3 feet 6 inches or a pool with a depth of 1.2 m?

8 Which is longer: 20 feet of cable or 7 m of cable?

HOMEWORK 22A

1   The table shows the time taken by 60 people to travel to work.

Time in minutes	10 or less	Between 10 and 30	30 or more
Frequency	8	19	33

Draw a pie chart to illustrate the data.

2   The table shows the number of GCSE passes that 180 students obtained.

GCSE passes	9 or more	7 or 8	5 or 6	4 or less
Frequency	20	100	50	10

Draw a pie chart to illustrate the data.

3   Tom is doing a Statistics project on the use of computers. He decides to do a survey to find out the main use of computers by 36 of his school friends. His results are shown in the table.

Mail use	e-mail	Internet	Word processing	Games
Frequency	5	13	3	15

  a   Draw a pie chart to illustrate his data.
  b   What conclusions can you draw from his data?
  c   Give reasons why Tom's data is not really suitable for his project.

★4   In a survey, a TV researcher asks 120 people at a Leisure Centre to name their favourite type of television programme. The results are shown in the table.

Type of programme	Comedy	Drama	Films	Soaps	Sport
Frequency	18	11	21	26	44

  a   Draw a pie chart to illustrate the data.
  b   Do you think the sample chosen by the researcher is representative of the population? Give a reason for your answer.

★5   Marion is writing an article on health for a magazine. She asked a sample of people the question: 'When planning your diet, do you consider your health?' The pie chart shows the results of her question.

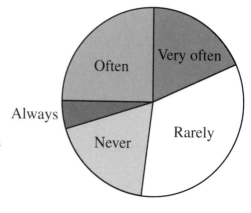

  a   What percentage of the sample responded 'often'.
  b   What response was given by about a third of the sample?
  c   Can you tell how many people there were in the sample? Give a reason for your answer.
  d   What other questions could Marion ask?

★1 The table below shows the heights and weights of twelve students in a class.

Student	Weight (Kg)	Height (cm)
Ann	51	123
Bridie	58	125
Ciri	57.5	127
Di	62	128
Emma	59.5	129
Flo	65	129
Gill	65	133
Hanna	65.5	135
Ivy	71	137
Joy	75.5	140
Keri	70	143
Laura	78	145

a Plot the data on a scatter diagram.
b Draw the line of best fit.
c Jayne was absent from the class, but they knew she was 132 cm tall. Use the line of best fit to estimate her weight.
d A new girl joined the class who weighed 55 kg. What height would you expect her to be?

★2 The table below shows the marks for ten pupils in their mathematics and music examinations.

Pupil	Maths	Music
Alex	52	50
Ben	42	52
Chris	65	60
Don	60	59
Ellie	77	61
Fan	83	74
Gary	78	64
Hazel	87	68
Irene	29	26
Jez	53	45

a Plot the data on a scatter diagram. Take the x-axis for the mathematics scores and mark it from 20 to 100. Take the y-axis for the music scores and mark it from 20 to 100.
b Draw the line of best fit.
c One of the pupils was ill when they took the music examination. Which pupil was it most likely to be?
d Another pupil, Kris, was absent for the music examination but scored 45 in mathematics, what mark would you expect him to have got in music?
e Another pupil, Lex, was absent for the mathematics examination but scored 78 in music, what mark would you expect him to have got in mathematics?

1   'People like the video hire centre to be open 24 hours a day.'
    a   To see whether this statement is true, design a data collection sheet which will allow
        you to capture data while standing outside a video hire centre.
    b   Does it matter at which time you collect your data?

2   The Youth Club wanted to know which types of activities it should plan, e.g. craft,
    swimming, squash, walking, disco etc.
    a   Design a data collection sheet which you could use to ask the pupils in your school
        which activities they would want in a Youth Club.
    b   Invent the first 30 entries on the chart.

★3 What types of film do your age group watch at the cinema the most? Is it comedy,
    romance, sci-fi, action, suspense or something else?
    a   Design a data collection sheet to be used in a survey of your age group.
    b   Invent the first thirty entries on your sheet.

Q HOMEWORK 22D

1   Design a questionnaire to test the following statement.
    'Young people aged 16 and under will not tell their parents when they have been drinking
    alcohol, but the over 16s will always let their parents know.'

★2 'Boys will use the Internet almost everyday but girls will only use it about once a week.'
    Design a questionnaire to test this statement.

★3 Design a questionnaire to test the following hypothesis.
    'When you are in your twenties, you watch less TV than any other age group.'

4   While on holiday in Wales, I noticed that in the supermarkets there were a lot more
    women than men, and even then, the only men I did see were over 65.
    a   Write down a hypothesis from the above observation.
    b   Design a questionnaire to test your hypothesis.

Chapter 23   Pattern

Q HOMEWORK 23A

Look for the pattern and then write the next two lines. Check your answers with a
calculator afterwards.

1   $7 \times 11 \times 13 \times 2 = 2002$
    $7 \times 11 \times 13 \times 3 = 3003$
    $7 \times 11 \times 13 \times 4 = 4004$
    $7 \times 11 \times 13 \times 5 = 5005$

2   $3 \times 7 \times 13 \times 37 \times 2 = 20202$
    $3 \times 7 \times 13 \times 37 \times 3 = 30303$
    $3 \times 7 \times 13 \times 37 \times 4 = 40404$
    $3 \times 7 \times 13 \times 37 \times 5 = 50505$

3
$3 \times 5 = 4^2 - 1 = 15$
$4 \times 6 = 5^2 - 1 = 24$
$5 \times 7 = 6^2 - 1 = 35$
$6 \times 8 = 7^2 - 1 = 48$

4
$3 \times 7 = 5^2 - 4 = 21$
$4 \times 8 = 6^2 - 4 = 32$
$5 \times 9 = 7^2 - 4 = 45$
$6 \times 10 = 8^2 - 4 = 60$

From your observations on the number patterns above, answer Questions **5** to **12** without using a calculator. Check with a calculator once you have attempted them.

5 $7 \times 11 \times 13 \times 9 =$

6 $3 \times 7 \times 13 \times 37 \times 8$

7 $99 \times 101 =$

8 $98 \times 102 =$

9 $7 \times 11 \times 13 \times 15 =$

10 $3 \times 7 \times 13 \times 37 \times 15 =$

11 $998 \times 1002 =$

12 $3 \times 7 \times 13 \times 37 \times 99 =$

HOMEWORK 23B

1 Look at the following number sequences. Write down the next three terms in each and explain how each sequence is found.
 a 4, 6, 8, 10, …
 b 3, 6, 9, 12, …
 c 2, 4, 8, 16, …
 d 5, 12, 19, 26, …
 e 3, 30, 300, 3000, …
 f 1, 4, 9, 16, …

2 Look carefully at each number sequence below. Find the next two numbers in the sequence and try to explain the pattern.
 a 1, 2, 3, 5, 8, 13, 21, …
 b 2, 3, 5, 8, 12, 17, …

3 Look at the sequences below. Find the rule for each sequence and write down its next three terms.
 a 7, 14, 28, 56, …
 b 3, 10, 17, 24, 31, …
 c 1, 3, 7, 15, 31, …
 d 40, 39, 37, 34, …
 e 3, 6, 11, 18, 27, …
 f 4, 5, 7, 10, 14, 19, …
 g 4, 6, 7, 9, 10, 12, …
 h 5, 8, 11, 14, 17, …
 i 5, 7, 10, 14, 19, 25, …
 j 10, 9, 7, 4, …
 k 200, 40, 8, 1.6, …
 l 3, 1.5, 0.75, 0.375, …

HOMEWORK 23C

1 Use each of the following rules to write down the first five terms of a sequence.
 a $3n + 1$ for $n = 1, 2, 3, 4, 5$
 b $2n - 1$ for $n = 1, 2, 3, 4, 5$
 c $4n + 2$ for $n = 1, 2, 3, 4, 5$
 d $2n^2$ for $n = 1, 2, 3, 4, 5$
 e $n^2 - 1$ for $n = 1, 2, 3, 4, 5$

2 Write down the first five terms of the sequence which has its nth term as
 a $n + 2$
 b $4n - 1$
 c $4n - 3$
 d $n^2 + 1$
 e $2n^2 + 1$

HOMEWORK 23D

1 Find the nth term in each of these linear sequences.
 a 5, 7, 9, 11, 13 …
 b 3, 7, 11, 15, 19, …
 c 6, 11, 16, 21, 26, …
 d 3, 9, 15, 21, 27, …
 e 4, 7, 10, 13, 16, …
 f 3, 10, 17, 24, 31, …

2 Find the 50th term in each of these linear sequences.

    a 3, 5, 7, 9, 11, …   **b** 5, 9, 13, 17, 21, …   **c** 8, 13, 18, 23, 28, …

    d 2, 8, 14, 20, 26, …   **e** 5, 8, 11, 14, 17, …   **f** 2, 9, 16, 23, 30, …

3 For each sequence **a** to **f**, find

    i the nth term   **ii** the 100th term   **iii** the term closest to 100

    a 4, 7, 10, 13, 16, …   **b** 7, 9, 11, 13, 15, …   **c** 3, 8, 13, 18, 23, …

    d 1, 5, 9, 13, 17, …   **e** 2, 10, 18, 26, …   **f** 5, 6, 7, 8, 9, …

 HOMEWORK 23E

1 A conference centre had tables each of which could sit 3 people. When put together, the tables could seat people as shown.

 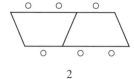 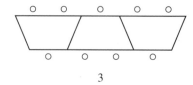

          1   2   3

    a How many people could be seated at 4 tables?

    b How many people could be seated at n tables put together in this way?

    c A conference had 50 people who wished to use the tables in this way. How many tables would they need?

2 A pattern of shapes is built up from matchsticks as shown.

  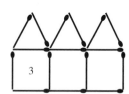

          1   2   3

    a Draw the 4th diagram.

    b How many matchsticks are in the nth diagram?

    c How many matchsticks are in the 25th diagram?

    d With 200 matchsticks, which is the biggest diagram that could be made?

3 A pattern of hexagons is built up from matchsticks.

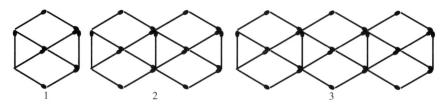

          1   2   3

    a Draw the 4th set of hexagons in this pattern.

    b How many matchsticks are needed for the nth set of hexagons?

    c How many matchsticks are needed to make the 60th set of hexagons?

    d If there are only 100 matchsticks, which is the largest set of hexagons that could be made?